AF556951

THE NATALIE AND IRVING FORMAN COLLECTION

THE NATALIE AND IRVING

FORMAN COLLECTION

An exhibition organized by
Karen Lee Spaulding with
Natalie and Irving Forman

With an essay by Lilly Wei
and foreword by Louis Grachos

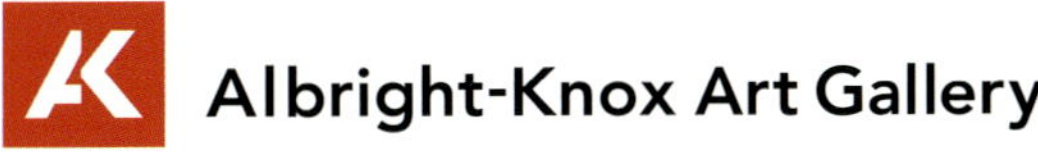

BUFFALO, NEW YORK

This exhibition is made possible through the generous support of The Margaret L. Wendt Foundation and Charles E. Balbach.

Albright-Knox Art Gallery
1285 Elmwood Avenue, Buffalo, New York 14222-1096

First Edition

Library of Congress
Cataloging-in-Publication Data

Albright-Knox Art Gallery.
The Natalie and Irving Forman collection: an exhibition/organized by Karen Lee Spaulding with Natalie and Irving Forman; with an essay by Lilly Wei and foreword by Louis Grachos. – 1st ed.
p. cm.
Catalog of an exhibition held at the Albright-Knox Art Gallery.
Includes bibliographical references and index.
ISBN 1-887457-04-6
1. Art, Abstract—Exhibitions. 2. Monochrome painting—Exhibitions. 3. Forman, Natalie—Art collections—Exhibitions. 4. Forman, Irving—Art collections—Exhibitions. 5. Art—New York (State)—Buffalo—Exhibitions. 6. Albright-Knox Art Gallery—Exhibitions. I. Spaulding, Karen Lee. II. Wei, Lilly. III. Grachos, Louis. IV. Title.

N6494.A2A43 2005
709'.04'04207474796—DC22 2005040970

Editor: Sarah Hezel
Design: Joseph Guglietti Design, Santa Fe, New Mexico
Print Management: Robert L. Freudenheim, Buffalo, New York
Printing: Transcontinental Printing, Québec City, Canada

CONTENTS

FOREWORD

IT IS WITH PRIDE AND GREAT PLEASURE that we present this exhibition and documentary catalogue in celebration of Natalie and Irving Forman's gift of their collection to the Albright-Knox Art Gallery. This is the single largest gift of artworks in the history of the Albright-Knox Art Gallery to have been donated at one time and one of the most remarkable for its relevance and significance to our collection of abstract art. A gift of this magnitude must be celebrated and shared, and it is with this special exhibition and publication that we honor and pay tribute to the Formans and their most generous gift to our community.

Natalie and Irving, each with an astute collector's eye and fueled by a shared passion, have brought together a brilliant collection of paintings, sculpture, and works on paper. The collection in its entirety is a magnificent representation of works by nearly fifty artists comprising 161 paintings and sculpture and 127 works on paper. Individually, each work presents an opportunity to examine an individual artist's particular approach to the nuances of color, structure, and materiality. As a whole, the collection provides opportunities for studying the endless manifestations of monochromatic abstraction. This most significant gift to the Gallery's permanent collection was mirrored by the equally remarkable gift of the Papers of Natalie and Irving Forman to the Albright-Knox Art Gallery Archives, G. Robert Strauss, Jr. Memorial Library, which will ensure that this invaluable resource is available to researchers, students, and scholars now and in the years to come.

It is an honor to have accepted, on behalf of the Albright-Knox Art Gallery, such an exceptional collection from two individuals whom I admire so greatly. To see the works of artists such as John Beech, Phil Sims, and Marcia Hafif take up residence beside the Albright-Knox Art Gallery's collection of masterworks by Josef Albers, Frank Stella, and Agnes Martin among others, is extremely gratifying. This major gift continues the Gallery's long tradition of generous patronage and bequests over the past 143 years, and we hope will serve as a catalyst for others.

Numerous individuals in both Buffalo and Santa Fe have played noteworthy roles in this extraordinary event. From The Buffalo Fine Arts Academy Board of Directors, I want particularly to thank Charles E. Balbach for providing seed money for this project and initiating the financial support for this publication and the exhibition. The leadership and support of Board President Charles W. Banta was also integral to the project. My deepest gratitude is extended also to the Margaret L. Wendt Foundation, notably Robert J. Kresse, Thomas D. Lunt, and Janet L. Day, for their ongoing support of the Gallery's activities and their role in making this exhibition and catalogue a reality.

My relationship with Natalie and Irving Forman and the eventual gifting of their collection to the Albright-Knox Art Gallery are due, in no small part, to Charlotte Jackson. I first met Natalie and Irving through Charlotte and her gallery in Santa Fe. She has been a steadfast advocate for the Formans and their collection, and I cannot thank her enough for the role she played in initiating this gift to Buffalo and the Albright-Knox.

Last, but not least, I extend my heartfelt thanks to Karen Lee Spaulding for leading and coordinating this project. She took on this assignment in addition to her duties as Deputy Director with incomparable grace and good humor. Her editorial expertise, keen eye for detail, and astute aesthetic judgment have resulted in an exhibition and catalogue fitting the magnitude and magnificence of the Formans' gift.

LOUIS GRACHOS
Director

ACKNOWLEDGMENTS

WHEN PROFESSIONAL ENDEAVORS intersect with personal enrichment and one's life passion, then work becomes the very best possible enterprise. When I was given the privilege of leading the effort of organizing this celebration of the extraordinary gift of the Natalie and Irving Forman Collection to the Albright-Knox Art Gallery, I knew that the pace would be breathless, the details countless, and the rewards enormous.

First and foremost, I extend special and profound gratitude to Louis Grachos, Director of the Albright-Knox Art Gallery. Louis instinctively knew that such a project would not only give me the opportunity to work with Natalie and Irving—for whom I hold the greatest respect, admiration, and affection—but would also bring me closer to being with works of art and plunge me back into my professional roots as an editor. I am indebted to him for all of that, for his professional generosity, and for his confidence in the work that I do on behalf of this institution.

Lilly Wei, art critic for *Art News* and *Art in America*, among many other publications, not only embraced our request to write the essay with alacrity, she also produced it with equal speed. We extend our gratitude to her for her willingness to participate and for her keen observations contained herein.

Projects such as this are clearly and emphatically a team effort. Marie-Françoise Hutchison, exhibition assistant extraordinaire, attended to every detail of every phase and aspect of the exhibition and its catalogue with good humor, organizational finesse, insight, and intelligence. Kelly Mullaney, Associate/Deputy Director's Office, is a partner in all things but in this regard especially, she has been indispensable in every matter having to do with the successful realization of the Forman project. Quite simply, I cannot thank them both enough for their focus, responsiveness, commitment, kindness, and for accommodating my frenetic schedule with such patience and grace.

The staff at the Gallery contributes in critical and important ways to making an exhibition possible. Preparation of the book you hold in your hands began well in advance of the exhibition opening. The Gallery's Research Resources team of Margaret Yacobucci and Pamela Jones, led by Head of Research Resources Susana Tejada, accomplished the research portion of the book in record time while maintaining impeccable standards. Special care and attention were provided by Head of Publications Sarah Hezel who worked with Marie-Françoise to prepare the manuscript and illustrative materials for publication, cleared permission rights, finalized every detail, and proofed every line countless times to ensure that the catalogue will serve as a sourcebook for the Forman Collection. Assistant Editor Robin Boyko edited and supervised the production of numerous complementary projects with great attentiveness. Yvonne Widenor and David Chan of the Image Resource Center provided invaluable service for the catalogue through digital imaging of the Forman works. Senior Curator Douglas Dreishpoon and Curatorial Assistant Kristen Carbone supported the effort with sage and expert advice. Mariann Smith, Curator of Education, and the staff of the Education Department conceived creative and innovative ways to engage our public in the nuances of monochromatic art. Chief Financial Officer Patrick Kilcullen and Controller Melissa Brainard provided sound management of the exhibition budget and kept us all on course. As well, Susan Griffin always made sure I had enough resources to get to Santa Fe and back, over and over again. The staff in the Membership / Development department worked to support and promote the exhibition in significant ways. Senior Registrar Laura Fleischmann provided important counsel in the preparatory stages of the exhibition and oversaw all conservation and transportation needs with proficiency and skill along with Associate Registrar Daisy

Stroud and Assistant Registrar Rebecca Endres, who worked on all the details of installation in their usual skilled way. Headed by Tim Short, the Buildings and Grounds department—Michael Dougherty, Tom Gallagher, and Ken Walker—worked their usual miracles and juggled the needs of three ambitious exhibitions simultaneously. Art Installers Ken Short and Gabriel Dunn made it possible for Natalie and Irving to install the exhibition with Louis in a way that was efficient and utterly enjoyable. Public Information Officer Cheryl Orlick and Marketing Consultant Maria Morreale collaborated on all aspects of promoting the exhibition so that the widest possible audience would have the opportunity to share in our celebration of this important gift to the permanent collection. Edward J.P. Drabczyk, Head of Security and Safety, worked with his team to ensure that the paintings were safe and protected. Jeff Fields, Candice Baller, and the entire Gallery Shop staff supported this exhibition through their enthusiasm for the works of art and through the complementary displays in the Shop. Events Coordinator Caterine Gatewood ensured that every detail of the celebratory weekend was perfect as she extended gracious hospitality to countless artists, gallery dealers, family friends of the Formans, and out-of-town guests to the Buffalo/Niagara region. They are—each and every one—wonderful colleagues, and they have my heartfelt appreciation.

In Buffalo, I had the enormous pleasure of working once again with Robert L. Freudenheim on the printing and production of the exhibition catalogue. Bob brought to the project the highest possible standards, and the results are self-evident. The Travel Team provided our guests with arrangements for a stellar tour of the cultural sights in Buffalo; special thanks go to Ronald Luczak and Maureen Watz for all that they did in that regard. My family, and particularly my husband Rick, were exceedingly understanding about the late nights, weekend work, and trips away from home to see this project to fruition.

Over the last two years, I have been fortunate enough to travel to Santa Fe numerous times to work on this exhibition. Charlotte Jackson, Sarah Deats, and Fiona MacConnell, of Charlotte Jackson Fine Art were cheerful partners in pulling together information and resource material on their end. Eddie Romero, family assistant to Natalie and Irving, became a fast, dear friend and willing colleague on late-night runs to Kinkos to prepare catalogue materials. Artists Erika Blumenfeld and Eric Tillinghast, both represented in the Forman Collection, were indispensable in working with me to catalogue and photograph nearly 170 individual works on paper during one trip. Alan Ebnother and Jennah Ward, also represented in the Collection, and Gabrielle Bakker, served as invaluable conservation resources in connection with the exhibition. Particular and special recognition goes to Joseph Guglietti, who designed this book with great sensitivity and a brilliant eye. He has been an exceptional collaborator, and I have enjoyed working with him on every page.

And to Natalie and Irving Forman: they welcomed me into their home with warmth and affection; they indulged my need to work nonstop on whirlwind two-day visits; they insisted on fun as a requisite part of each stay; they cooked and served the most glorious meals with abandon, and most of all, they shared their passion for their collection and their insights into the creative process every minute of every day. It has been an indelible pleasure to spend such precious time with them.

KAREN LEE SPAULDING
Deputy Director

TRUE COLORS

THE NATALIE AND IRVING FORMAN COLLECTION OF PAINTING AND SCULPTURE

Our task is not to find the maximum amount of content in a work of art, much less to squeeze more content out of the work than is already there. Our task is to cut back content so that we can see the thing at all.[1]

–Susan Sontag

"THE MONOCHROME PAINTING IS THE MOST MYSTERIOUS ICON OF MODERN ART."

So begins critic Thomas McEvilley's first essay, "Seeing the Primal through Paint, The Monochrome Icon" in *The Exile's Return*, a provocative critique of painting in postmodernist times, published in 1993. He describes this imagined scene:

> A rectangle of a single more or less unmodulated color is erected on the wall at eye level and gazed at by humans standing before it in a reverential silence. What is happening? The painting is not impressing the viewer through a display of skill. In it, skill is negated. Draughtsmanship is negated. Compositional sense is negated. Color manipulation and relationship are negated. Subject matter, drama, narrative, painterly presence, touch are absent. The color may have been applied with a roller or spray gun; it may even be the natural color of the unpainted fabric. One might as well be looking at the wall the picture is mounted on. Yet here, in this ritual-pictorial moment, the deepest meanings of Western Modernist art are embedded—its highest spiritual aspirations, its dream of a utopian future, its madness, its folly.[2]

McEvilley has presented a not uncharacteristic list of monochome's perceived failings. This is how monochrome painting has often been judged, as a series of negatives, as paintings that are not only reductive but reductive to the point of inertness, evaluated as (outmoded) historical, philosophic, or aesthetic ideas. It is curious that this ostensibly most visual and egalitarian form of painting, one that requires least in the way of erudition for response and interpretation—although erudition may deepen appreciation—has become the emblem of elitist art, even an anti-art or anti-painting, to be experienced cerebrally rather than viscerally. Depending upon the viewer's sensibility and sensitivity to color, shape, light, texture, and so on, monochrome has been apotheosized for its purity and utopianism or vilified for its aloofness, arrogance, and self-delusion. It has been praised and dismissed for its literalism. Called, at times, a ground waiting for an image, it provokes skepticism and disdain because it looks too easy, anger because it seems to be a joke at the viewer's expense, unease and inadequacy because the viewer finds it impenetrable, or boredom because we are more and more conditioned to expect quick takes, multiplicity, and excess, to fireworks and explosions, bells and whistles.

Yet, let us look at this "rectangle" more closely, like those rapt and reverent humans whom McEvilley posits. Indeed, if they are looking closely, with or without reverence, they might see more. Take, for instance, the designation "single" color. While true monochrome is defined as one-color painting, there are very few true monochromes in existence. In fact, so-called monochrome painters seldom use only one color to make their paintings. Many use a wide array of hues despite the surface color, which may appear singular. However, that singularity is often the result of layers of different colors—ten, twenty, thirty, 300, or more—to obtain the desired result, the invented color, the specific light. There is also the question of what constitutes a single color in a monochromatic painting. Uninflected color, to be sure, and color toned from dark to light or light to dark is usually thought of as a single color. However, can the wide variations on blue, say, each with its own name, its own infinite tonal scale, mixed with other hues, warmed and cooled, but still recognizably blue be reckoned as one color? When all those differently mixed blues are applied to one painting, is that painting truly monochromatic?

"More or less unmodulated" color is next on the list. Monochrome works are often modulated—if modulation is understood to be the adjusting of tonalities—in order to establish other painterly effects, like movement, space, density, weight, shape, light, and surface patterns. Lack of skill is also noted, which is an even more common misrepresentation. A great deal of skill, knowledge, and labor goes into monochrome painting; it is hardly ever the slapping on of one layer of house paint—and even that requires a degree of skill. A command of color theory and practice is present, as well as an understanding of light and its properties and the physiology and psychology of perception. Draughtsmanship is not necessarily dispensed with, just draughtsmanship in the service of mimesis. Nor are compositional sense, color manipulation, and relationship lacking. They just appear with less apparent differentiation and perhaps less immediate visibility. It is also thought that subject matter, drama, narrative, painterly presence, and touch are absent, but as in any other kind of painting, that depends upon the painter. In content, monochrome works can refer to the spiritual and the transcendent or they can be literal, the content their materials and process, the thing in itself. Touch, decried by minimalism, also depends upon the artist, whether it is emphasized, the surface roiled and made distinctive with signature markings or smoothed over and depersonalized, originality and subjective prerogatives refused. The application is, as with any painter, various: brushed, spray gunned, rollered, rubbed, dripped, splattered and yes, unpainted canvas may be utilized. But less is not nothing and may not even be less. The penultimate allegation states that there is little, at times, that distinguishes a monochrome painting from the wall it hangs on but this is hardly ever true although certain monochromes depend upon a more tightly integrated relationship to the wall and to the architectural space than other kinds of art.

To speak of monochrome paintings in general is to ignore the individuality of both monochromatic artists and their works but more often than not, this is what occurs. More than most stylistic groupings, it tends to be thought of as monolithic. But it cannot be emphasized enough that all monochromes are not the same and the distinctions and criteria that apply to other kinds of paintings apply to it. As an Arshile Gorky painting is not a Willem de Kooning, an Ad Reinhardt is not a Robert Ryman, and an Yves Klein is not a Rudolf de Crignis.

The Natalie and Irving Forman Collection of Painting and Sculpture and a trove of works on paper are a selection of mainly monochromatic art—Josef Albers, Burgoyne Diller, Mark di Suvero, and Leon Polk Smith are some exceptions—acquired object by object with passionate discernment and the knowledge and sensibility accumulated through a lifetime of dedicated looking. When the Formans moved to Santa Fe from Chicago in 1985, they began yet another collection; the previous had been given to the Art Institute of Chicago; Museum of Contemporary Art, Chicago; Milwaukee Art Museum; University of California, Berkeley Art Museum; and other eminent institutions. This effort was a continuation of their earlier interests, which was spurred by a profound love for the paintings of Mark Rothko, Clyfford Still, Barnett Newman, and Ad Reinhardt, (they owned several of the latter at one point) and for constructivist art and the processes of painting. More than amassing monochromatic or minimalist art as a stylistic imperative, the Formans bought what they deeply loved and wanted to live with. Nonetheless, they were also driven by a keen desire to possess works that would represent an integral sequence of contemporary art with relevance for future generations.

It is a lucid and elegant collection that presses home the sheer, unmediated beauty and dazzle of color in all of its infinite variety as an affective visual and tactile experience. Multi-generational, for the most part intimate in scale as befits a private collection (although some pieces are quite large), it represents approximately fifty artists with the bulk of the work dating from the 1980s and 1990s. Consisting of 161 paintings and sculptures—but mostly paintings—the Albright-Knox now has the most extensive collection of monochromes in this country, and the fact that it can be seen together in one location is of supreme importance. Monochromes must be experienced face to face. In reproduction, they are merely notational, colored postage stamps, little rectangles and squares on a page, points of reference, not a fact, not visually resonant. Part of the ongoing history of the monochrome, this collection is an insight into what might still be possible after monochrome's absolutism, re-shaped by present times, has ceded to more contingent, relativist interpretations that acknowledge, to some extent, color's social and political implications. The range of art here encompasses the metaphysical, the formalist, the materialist, most often as a mix of all three, reflecting our more catcgorically fluid, hybridized times. These are the descendants of both Malevich's art of transcendence—with an occasional detour through Buddhism—and the "real materials in real space" of the constructivists.[3] By the 1950s, monochrome had established itself as one of the most exemplary of modernist images, identified with artists such as Lucio Fontana, Ellsworth Kelly, Yves Klein, Piero Manzoni, Barnett Newman, Ad Reinhardt, and Mark Rothko. But modernism faltered, as the Hegelian model of progress collapsed, and with it the idea that Western civilization was perfectible, inevitably advancing toward utopia, that culture could trump nature. From the mid-1960s until the early 1980s, a

severe reaction against modernism and the modernist program swept in, and painting, as the modernist medium par excellence, was toppled in the onrush of other paradigms.[4] Reinhardt, who famously said, "I am simply making the last paintings which can ever be made" kept painting his black paintings from 1955 until his death in 1967, a restatement of Aleksandr Rodchenko's 1921 proclamation, in which he declared the death of painting; "it's all over" after painting a red monochrome, blue monochrome, and yellow monochrome. However, monochrome, considered to be the end of painting, like painting itself, proved more durable.

The Forman Collection is essentially a collection of American artists although many enjoy a greater reputation in Europe than here, where monochrome has a stronger tradition, and its role in postmodernist strategies and discourse is still under assessment. The artists in the collection are more or less equally divided between east and west coasts and several Bay-area artists are represented in depth, such as John Meyer and David Simpson. There are also a few German monochromatists in the group: Heiner Thiel, who makes anodized aluminum and steel reliefs, intermediate between painting and sculpture; Peter Tollens, a traditionalist in terms of material, who uses egg tempera and oil on wood panel for his small-scale works; and Dieter Villinger, a high-voltage colorist. There are several artists who make objects from steel, such as Tom Waldron, as seen in his modestly sized, black steel geometric sculpture with gently curved surfaces and edges or Eric Tillinghast and his harder-edged, more regular, repeating forms.

The older artists, such as Stuart Arends, Joe Barnes, Mala Breuer, Rodney Carswell, Constance DeJong, Allan Graham, Gloria Graham, James Hayward, Florence Pierce, and Roy Thurston were, for the most part, formed by the art and aesthetic discourses of the 1950s, 1960s, and 1970s, from the transcendent aspirations of abstract expressionism, the high formalism of Clement Greenberg, and the systemic or serial objectivity of minimalism to the process-oriented art of post-minimalism. James Hayward, with his churning, thickly impastoed surfaces is one of the most gestural artists in the collection, and Florence Pierce, born in 1918, an original member of the Taos Transcendental Painting Group, 1938–1942, is represented by several glowing, resin reliefs on mirrored Plexiglas from the 1990s that look remarkably fresh. Roy Thurston's lacquered and polyurethaned paintings attest to the latent power of reticence while Rodney Carswell's finely surfaced, red-rimmed white circle, 1991 (P. 53), for instance, plays with conceptual and perceptual tropes, with shape and color, figure and ground, and can also be read as *Red Circle/White Center*, the title of the work.

They are balanced by artists who came of age during the late 1970s, 1980s, and 1990s, informed by pluralism, hybridization, and more syncretic orientations, such as John Beech, Tom Benson, Erika Blumenfeld, Alan Ebnother, James Hyde, Rachel Lachowicz, Ed Malina, Patricia Moisan,

KAZIMIR MALEVICH

Suprematist Composition: White on White, 1918, Oil on canvas, 31¼ x 31¼ in. (78.7 x 78.7 cm.)

Collection The Museum of Modern Art, New York

Acquisition confirmed in 1999 by agreement with the Estate of Kazimir Malevich and made possible with funds from the Mrs. John Hay Whitney Bequest (by exchange) and Michael Rouillard. These younger artists hold less exalted ideas about monochrome and eagerly experimented with a greater range of materials in more radical juxtapositions. Their notion of monochrome embraced the world instead of rejecting it, and they did not necessarily limit themselves to an exclusively monochromatic stance. James Hyde is represented by a wonderfully crusty small fresco on Styrofoam, 1993 (P. 78), and Rachel Lachowicz by a little, silkily dense, gender-inflected canvas covered with lipstick, 2003 (P. 79). Michael Rouillard, who advocates structure and support, installation and architecture more than he does surface and color, is represented by three immaculately clean panels of white outlined in yellow pinned together to form a vertical sequence, 2001 (P. 111), a smooth Prussian blue rectangle; and a cadmium yellow one, both 1994 (PP. 109 AND 110), of acrylic on Plexiglas backed by an aluminum brace. John Beech is represented by a number of glue paintings that have the richness of encaustic, among other works. Beech is addicted to junk and prefers to use overlooked, cast-off utilitarian objects and materials with shapes and structures that catch his eye. Through color and inventive combinations, he reclaims and redefines them. *Large Elmer Painting*, 1993–1995, 2000 (P. 39), is a more than six-foot vertical rectangle, its golden radiance the result of glue and turmeric while several smaller glue works are three-dimensional, including the ruddy *Bent Glue Painting*, 2002 (P. 43), and *Glue Painting #59*, 2004 (P. 46), a minimalist-like fudge brown cube that is reminiscent of Donald Judd's work, except it is not quite so "specific" an object, its surface yielding, hand-made rather than industrially fabricated, its presence wryly understated, playfully ironic rather than implacably authoritative. Beech notes—with an attitude that is both demythicizing and demystifying—that "the finished piece is open-ended, still just a beginning in one sense. It could always be coated once more."[5]

For a majority of the artists in the Forman Collection, color is the subject, often in conjunction with light. Joe Barnes, a practicing Buddhist who made only white paintings from the 1970s until the early 1990s, now employs a full array of luminous, auratic shades. Barnes prefers a small format to focus and intensify the hue in order to offer the viewer a concentrated experience, a heightened but effortless awareness that leads to seeing more deeply and clearly. David Simpson has been an abstract artist since the 1950s but it was only in 1987 that he embraced the monochrome when he discovered a new medium: acrylic paint mixed with titanium dioxide-coated mica particles that create an iridescent effect. Combining complementaries, Simpson's metallic pigments create lightning fields of colors that shift depending upon the viewer's position vis-à-vis the surface. Phil Sims once stated that "for the painter, there can be no idea but in paint," an echo of William Carlos Williams's "no ideas but in things."[6] Sims's deft interplay of plus-and-minus markings resonates throughout the surface in a kind of kinetic tremor that subtly ripples the color. By adding clay to paint, his colors acquire a slightly matte finish that makes

YVES KLEIN

IKB 79, 1959, Acrylic on fabric and wood, 55 x 47 ⅛ in. (139.7 x 119.7 cm.)

Collection Tate Gallery, London, Great Britain

Purchased from the Galleria Internazionale and Situation (Grant-in-Aid) 1972

them denser, earthier, and more immediate. An original participant in the Radical Painting group, his saturated canvases have become increasingly voluptuous in recent works.

While some of the artists in this group might disavow the designation monochrome—or at least a strict interpretation of it, Joseph Marioni insists that he is a one-color painter. His richly hued canvases are typically called *Blue Painting*, 1997 (P. 172); *Red Painting*, 1995 (P. 84); *Green Painting*, 1996 (P. 85); *Yellow Painting*, 1997 (P. 87), and so on, a kind of gravity's rainbow of specific color, the paint applied in several layers by roller, which is permitted to flow downward. They reveal both the essential elements of painting and an integration of those elements: color, the color's vehicle, and the support. Marioni, who frequently writes on monochrome painting, was also an original member of the Radical Painting group that met in New York in the late 1970s and early 1980s.[7] He stated in his manifesto for radical painting, "Outside the Cartouche," 1986, written in collaboration with Günter Umberg, a German monochrome artist, that while monochrome presents the least information, it provides the most sensation of all painting. Besides that of color—or paint, "this kind of painting is not intended to associate with or present some other experience."[8] He ambitiously claimed that "each painting is a solution that is informed by its own time and location… and the painter involved in the investigation of the radical painting seeks an understanding of painting that will fit the entire history of painting."[9]

On the other hand, there are artists represented here who are not particularly invested in color as such. Rudolf de Crignis, a Swiss-born artist, represented in the Forman Collection by several "ultramarine" blue canvases, states that his work is premised on seeing and experiencing light; he is not interested in color except as a vehicle.[10] Critic Stefan Kraus notes that although "the color blue has dominated the immediate perception of de Crignis' work for a number of years," it is only a surface color, a "filter" or "catalyst" carefully built up in numerous layers so that the painting is actually three-dimensional and "vibrates" upon extended viewing, which also intensifies the color.[11] De Crignis prides himself on the construction of light solely through color, without technology, without the aid of costly, complicated electronic equipment. Another critic, Stefan Gronert, wrote that de Crignis's work is never truly about color but about more fundamental questions concerning instability, process, and the unavailability of the visible.[12] Of his paintings, with their miraculous, seemingly mark-free surfaces, de Crignis has said that visibility becomes a kind of event, one that requires the concentrated participation of the viewer.[13] Eventually, the gaze penetrates the fine mesh of his almost imperceptible strokings to enter into both an actual and perceptual zone of light and an immeasurable space.

Winston Roeth's paintings in the Forman Collection are distinctive for the band that surrounds them, a signature format that stretches the color expanse to the edge and holds it there. Roeth

AD REINHARDT

Abstract Painting No. 5, 1962, Oil on canvas, 60⅛ x 60⅛ in. (152.8 x 152.8 cm.)

Collection Tate Gallery, London, Great Britain

Presented by Mrs. Rita Reinhardt through the American Federation of Arts, 1972

says he follows the form of the painting in order to emphasize the interior. *Luzerne*, 1994 (P. 106), a red square edged in black; *Dark 3 x 4*, 1995 (P. 107), a matte, deep grey-blue rectangle rimmed by a livelier dark, a black-green that shifts in hue; and *Dreamer*, 2002 (P. 108), a horizontal rectangle of pristine yellow enclosed by gold—a more active, glowing yellow, a light—inspired by a dream of Irving Forman. Remarkable for the refinement of his surfaces, Roeth builds up countless layers of tempera in these paintings to achieve a chromatic density that traps light and creates a work with both flatness and depth. The pioneering minimalist collector Giuseppe Panza di Biumo, who counts many works by Roeth in his collection, as well as the work of several other artists in the Forman Collection, described Roeth's paintings as "atmospheres, not objects, nor surfaces. His paintings disappear in a bright, saturated vibration."[14]

James Howell also arrives at light and space in terms of the phenomena of surface, the glow emanating outward. Based on an ongoing and extensive study of grays, Howell's paintings, always in progressions, consist of narrow horizontal bands that may vary from series to series but are uniform in size throughout the works of any given suite. His bands are graduated in carefully calculated, subtly differentiated shades of gray that can be plotted along a parabolic curve. Howell is a methodical painter, and while he certainly qualifies as a pure monochromatist, he tempers his titanium white and ivory black with raw umber. With their barely perceptible differences, his exquisitely calibrated paintings probe perceptual limits, testing the sensitivity of the human eye and the engagement of the viewer.

Other artists are deeply involved with process and materials. John Meyer's painstakingly and gorgeously constructed single panels, diptychs and triptychs from 1985 to 2002, the year of his untimely death, are well represented. Using traditional mediums such as egg tempera, lacquer, oil, ground lapis lazuli, rice paper, fine-wood supports, Meyer aspired to contemporary paintings without the loss of traditional craft and materials. His works are unassuming at first glance but in time, their taut surfaces, composed of layers and layers of burnished color, reveal their richness. Delicate in appearance, they address perceptual shifts, the brevity of image and the relativity of color. Meyer once said that they were "not 'color' painting but 'colored' painting with no corporeal trace, no mark since the painting as a whole is the mark. They are not a writing or a narrative but a mist meeting a surface—just visual."[15]

Marcia Hafif's paintings are among the closest to pure monochrome there is and she, too, at times uses more than one color to construct her "one" color works. Hafif also inflects the surface although that inflection is the result of her matter-of-fact application, without expressive intent. Squares or just-off squares, Hafif's paintings are titled by the color used in the painting with the intent of full disclosure: here, for example, *French Painting: Terraile*, 1990 (P. 69), a

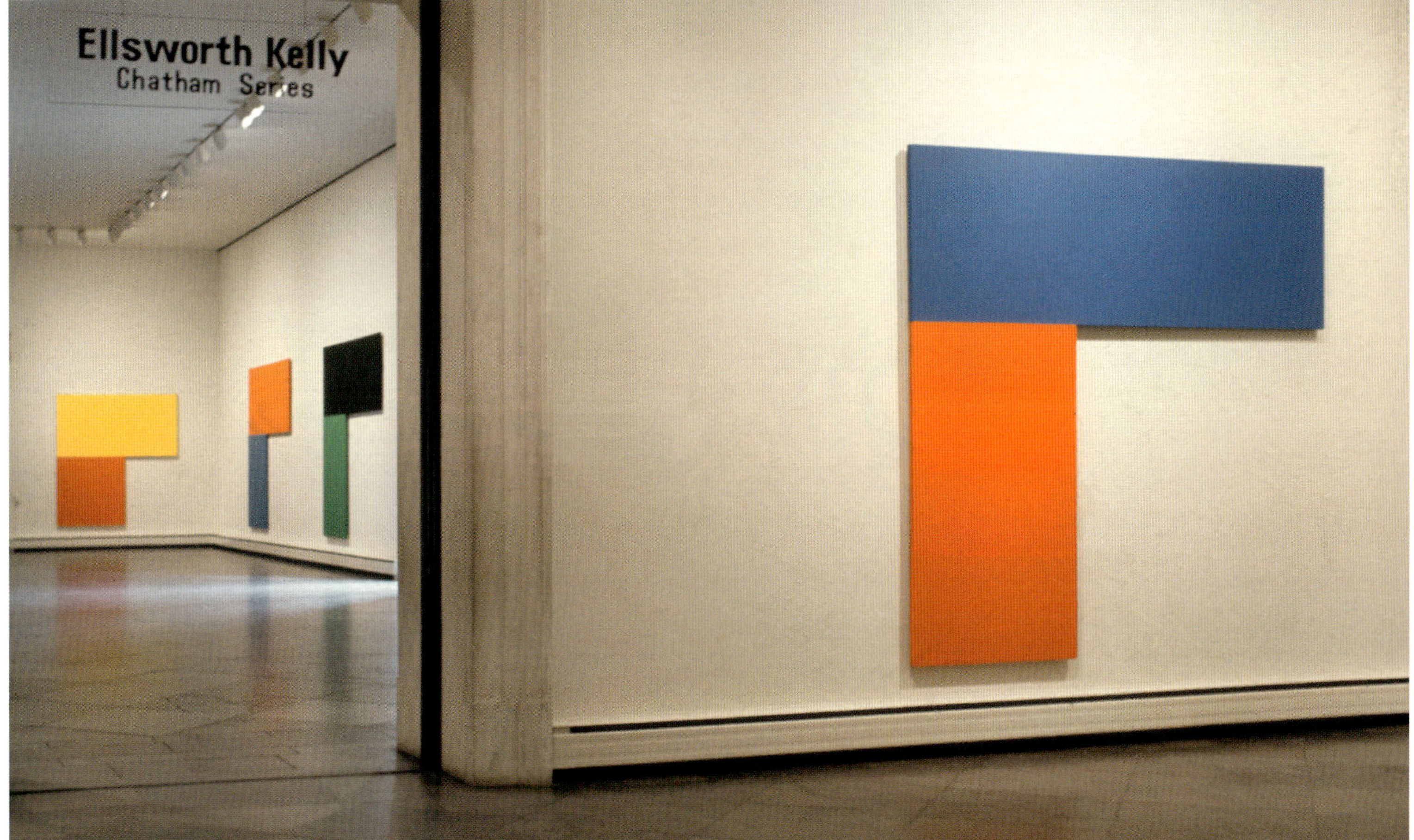
Ellsworth Kelly
Chatham Series

radiant pink; *Red Painting: Paliogen Maroon*, 1998 (P. 71); *Red Painting: Indian Yellow Tint*, 1998 (P. 70). Her project is to explore the making of a painting, from grinding the pigment into oil, fixing scale, proportion, mark, determining the medium—oil, encaustic, egg tempera, casein, glazes—frequently working with colors in a tonal sequence, a scale of flesh tints, say. She continues to look for ways to make paintings without complicated craft, based in part on the non-hierarchical, non-authorial concepts of the 1960s and 1970s. Yet, however pragmatically executed, Hafif's paintings are perceptually elusive, as color always is. Hafif once stated that they stand in for traditional paintings that can no longer be made.

Hafif has also discussed what she believes monochrome painting to be, a formulation that is quite different than Marioni's. In "Getting On with Painting," an article she wrote in 1981, Hafif said, "The meaning, then, of one-color painting is closely related to the act of painting, the action of painting. As it presently functions, this type of painting is neither a means of representation of nature nor is its purpose the 'self-expression' of the artist. It is, rather, a direct mode of thought by which the artist, using reason and intuition, works out (creates) meaning through his/her materials and through the process of using them."[16] She continues to say that its purpose is not reductive or analytical for its own sake but in the service of the development of a personal and poetic, specifically visual language. The strokes of painting do matter. Elaborating further, she includes non-verbal thought with rational thought in order to encompass the unintentional and the unknown. Painting, according to Hafif, functions as a source of identity as painters work through painting to the discovery of the self and the "artist produces work which has an exterior, public existence, but which also clarifies his internal sense of identity and forms a bridge to reality."[17]

In her essay, "Beginning Again," written in 1978, Hafif concludes: that "If one phase of this period of analysis [of non-objective painting] is coming to an end, we may be ready to enter still another phase of abstraction, a synthetic period."[18] The great significance of the Forman Collection is that it shows us what this synthetic phase of monochrome might look like, not as an end but another beginning, divested of myth if not meaning and allure, in which the hundreds, arguably thousands, of colors the human eye can register and the infinite complexity of that registration are enough to offset the essential simplicity of the monochrome ethos.

LILLY WEI

NOTES

1 Susan Sontag, *Against Interpretation and Other Essays* (New York: Farrar Straus Giroux, 1986) 14.

2 Thomas McEvilley, *The Exile's Return: Toward a Redefinition of Painting for the Post-Modern Era* (New York: Cambridge University Press, 1993) 9. Here, in a very abbreviated version, McEvilley describes the evolution of the non-objective monochrome thusly: "In the late eighteenth and nineteenth centuries the sublime in the visual arts was conceived primarily as a landscape theme: the awesome vastness of nature towering over the simultaneously exalted and intimated human observer... As the figure shrinks on the canvas, the vast surround of the universe is terrifyingly revealed. Behind such paintings lurks the Hegelian dread of culture, dissolving into the vast irrationality or valuelessness of nature, of the dream of civilization's advance sinking into the swamp. The fascination with the sublime progressively ate away at the figure and hypostatized the activated ground. In the twentieth century, it devolved finally on the monochrome surface, the pure ground into which all figures have dissolved, as its central icon, representing the blank of the erased cultural world or the blissful sleep of the soul which has returned to the One." 12.

3 See Camilla Gray's discussion of the suprematists and the constructivists in *The Great Experiment: Russian Art 1863–1922* (London: Thames and Hudson, 1962) reprinted edition, 1976, 131-219.

4 See McEvilley's explanations for the disappearance of painting during those years, before the return in the 1980s with neo-expressionism and the new abstraction in *The Exile's Return: Toward a Redefinition of Painting for the Post-Modern Era*, 9-64.

5 John Beech to the author in an email dated January 4, 2005.

6 *Radical Painting*, exh. cat., (Williamstown, MA: Williams College Museum of Art, 1984) 37.

7 The group consisted of a loose affiliation of "monochrome" painters who met in each other's studios and exhibited together in various permutations from around 1978 to 1983. It was founded by Marcia Hafif and Olivier Mosset as an informal forum to discuss monochrome issues, such as its relationship to current painting and also to discuss exhibitions for their work. Artists who participated at one time or another included Raimund Girke, Dale Henry, Alan Kleiman, Anders Knutsson, Allan McCollum, Joseph Marioni, Carmengloria Morales, Stephen Rosenthal, Robert Ryman, Doug Sanderson, Phil Sims, Howard Smith, Susanna Tanger, Frederic Matys Thursz, Günter Umberg, Merrill Wagner, and Jerry Zeniuk. In one of the planning sessions for the 1984 Williams College Museum of Art monochrome exhibition, organized by then director Thomas Krens, the term "radical painting" was coined by Zeniuk. Consequently, the exhibition was titled *Radical Painting* but it was essentially the end of the group; there were too many irresolvable differences among the artists, aesthetic and otherwise. "Radical painting" was then taken up by Marioni and Umberg and under its banner, they curated a number of monochromatic exhibitions, mostly in Europe.

8 Joseph Marioni and Günter Umberg, "Outside the Cartouche: The Question of the View in Radical Painting," in Joseph Marioni, *On the Right to Painting* (New York, 1998) 5, quoted in Barry Schwabsky, "Colors and Their Names," *Art in America*, June 1999, 89.

9 Ibid., Marioni and Umberg, 1, 8.

10 As for his "blue," the paintings in the Forman Collection consist of more than one blue, for instance, *Painting #96.9*, 1996 (P. 57), is ultramarine blue and royal blue; *Painting #98.7*, 1998 (P. 58), is Scheveninge green, ultramarine blue, and royal blue; and *Painting #01.37*, 2001 (P. 59), is flesh, ochre, flesh tint, pthalo turquoise, pale ultramarine blue, and royal blue.

11 Stefan Kraus, Studies in *Painting, 5.7.-26.8.2001* (Cologne, Germany: Artothek, 2001) 21.

12 Stefan Gronert, *Das Ereignis der Sichtbarkeit* (The Event of Visibility), 1999, publication forthcoming.

13 Rudolf de Crignis, *Rudolf de Crignis, 5 Paintings = 1 Work*, exh. cat. (Bonn, Germany: Kunstmuseum Bonn, 2003) unpaginated, frontispiece notes.

14 Giuseppe Panza di Biumo, quoted in Angela Madesani, *Storie di Colore* (Stories of Color), exh. cat. (Palazzo Libera, Villa Ligarina, Nicolodi Editori, Mantova, 2005) unpaginated.

15 Lilly Wei, "Framing the Diaphane, The Paintings of John Meyer," in *Fucare: To Paint Red*, exh. cat. (San Francisco: published by John Meyer, 1986), unpaginated.

16 Marcia Hafif, "Getting on with Painting," *Art in America*, April 1981, 133.

17 Ibid., 134.

18 Marcia Hafif, "Beginning Again," *Artforum*, September 1978, 40.

WORKS IN THE EXHIBITION

PLATES

PETER AGOSTINI

JOSEF ALBERS

TIMOTHY APP

STUART ARENDS

JOE BARNES

JOHN BEECH

TOM BENSON

ERIKA BLUMENFELD

MALA BREUER

RODNEY CARSWELL

JOHN CHAMBERLAIN

MARK COLE

JOHN CONNELL

RUDOLF DE CRIGNIS

CONSTANCE DEJONG

BURGOYNE DILLER

MARK DI SUVERO

ALAN EBNOTHER

ALLAN GRAHAM

GLORIA GRAHAM

MARCIA HAFIF

JAMES HAYWARD

JAMES HOWELL

JAMES HYDE

RACHEL LACHOWICZ

JODY LOMBERG

ED MALINA

JOSEPH MARIONI

ALLAN MCCOLLUM

JOHN MEYER

PATRICIA MOISAN

DOUG OHLSON

FLORENCE PIERCE

WINSTON ROETH

MICHAEL ROUILLARD

DAVID SIMPSON

PHIL SIMS

LEON POLK SMITH

HEINER THIEL

ROY THURSTON

ROBERT TIEMANN

ERIC TILLINGHAST

PETER TOLLENS

DIETER VILLINGER

TOM WALDRON

ALAN WAYNE

JOAN WITEK

PETER YOUNG

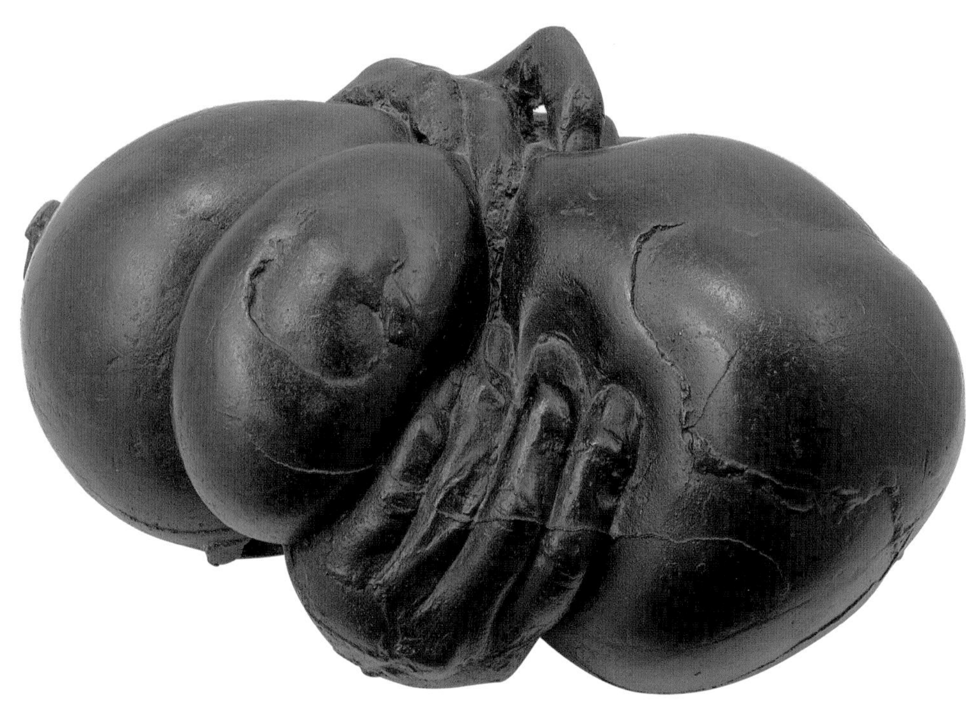

PETER AGOSTINI *Squeeze,* 1963
Bronze, 7 x 14 x 10 inches

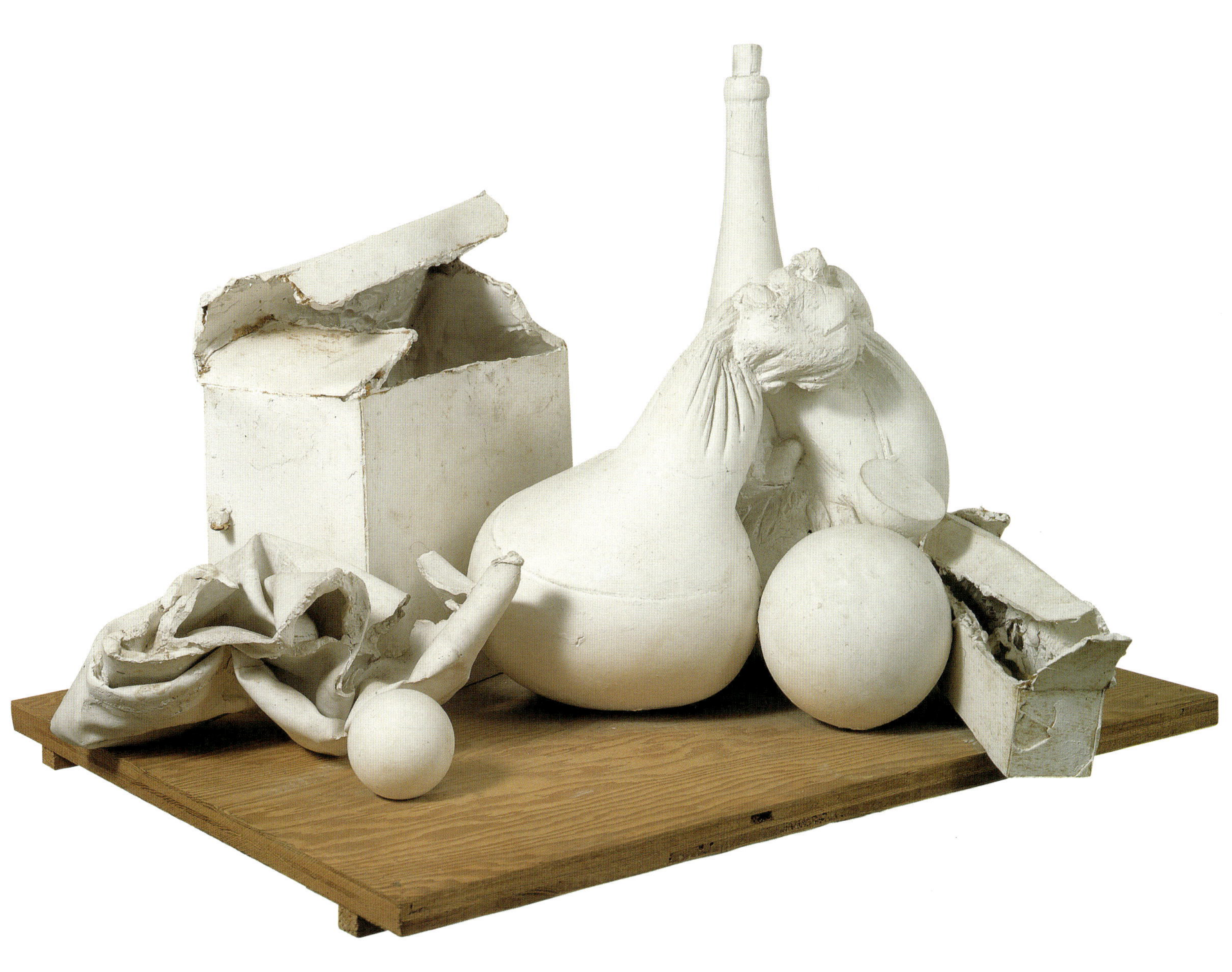

PETER AGOSTINI *Still Life #1,* 1964
Hydrocal, 15 x 23 x 22 inches

JOSEF ALBERS *Homage to the Square: Unexpected,* 1961
Oil on canvas mounted on board, 30 x 30 inches

TIMOTHY APP *Autumnal Light,* 1980
Oil on canvas, 40½ x 32⅛ inches

STUART ARENDS *Celadon 10,* 1989
Latex and wax on fiberboard, 48 x 48 x 6 inches

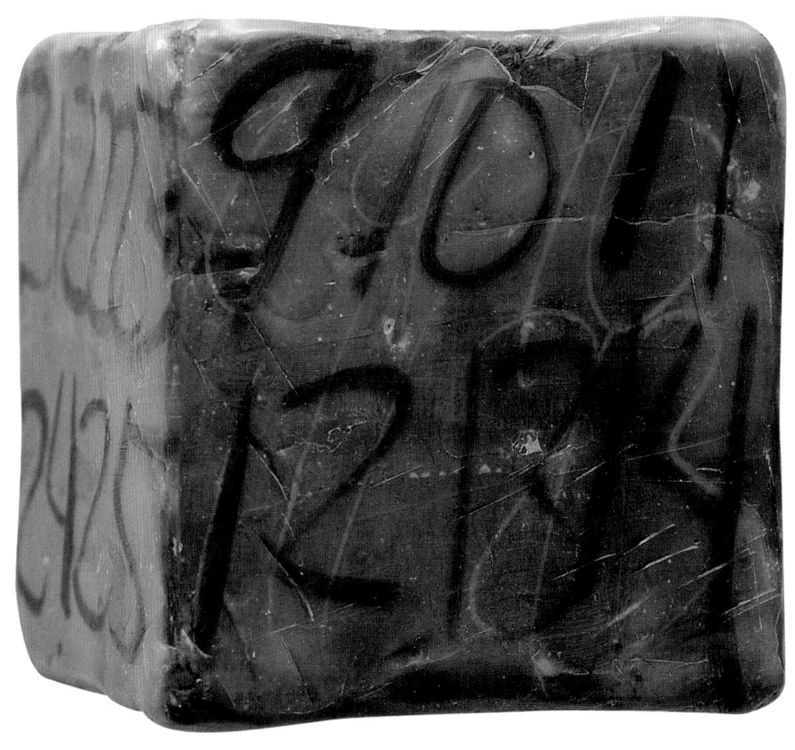

STUART ARENDS *C.W.8,* 1992
Oil and wax on wood, 3 ⅝ x 3 ⅝ x 3½ inches

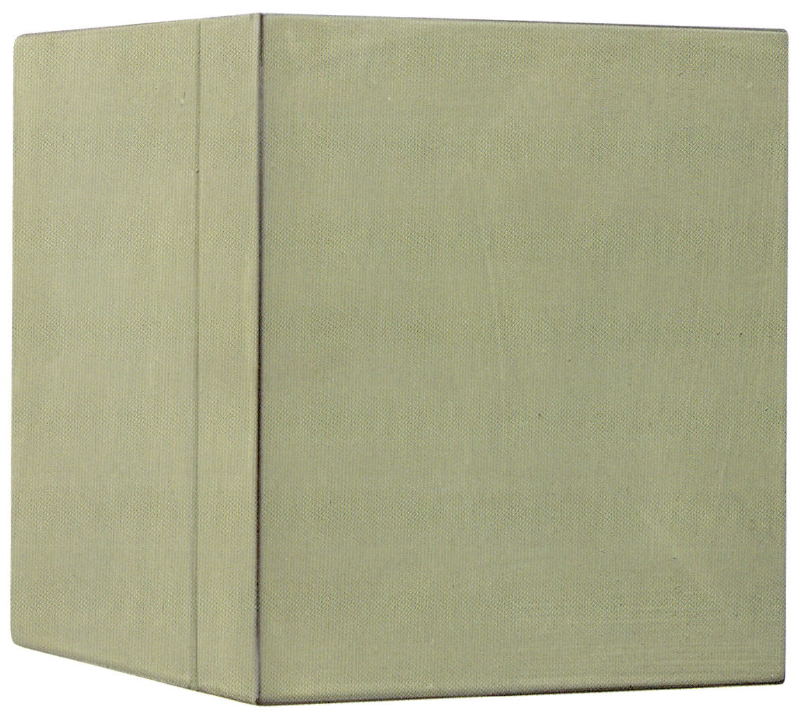

STUART ARENDS *O.S. 30,* 1993
Oil on steel, 3½ x 3½ x 3¼ inches

JOE BARNES *Not titled [4]*, 1995
Oil on canvas, 68 x 72 inches

JOE BARNES *Not titled,* 1997
Acrylic on canvas, 24 x 22½ inches

JOE BARNES *Not titled [chromium green oxide]*, 1997
Acrylic on canvas, 24 x 22½ inches

JOHN BEECH *Contact Glue Painting*, 1993
Contact cement on particleboard, 11 3/8 x 11 3/8 inches

JOHN BEECH *Large Elmer Painting,* 1993–1995, 2000
Glue and turmeric on fiberboard, 77½ x 35 x 3 inches

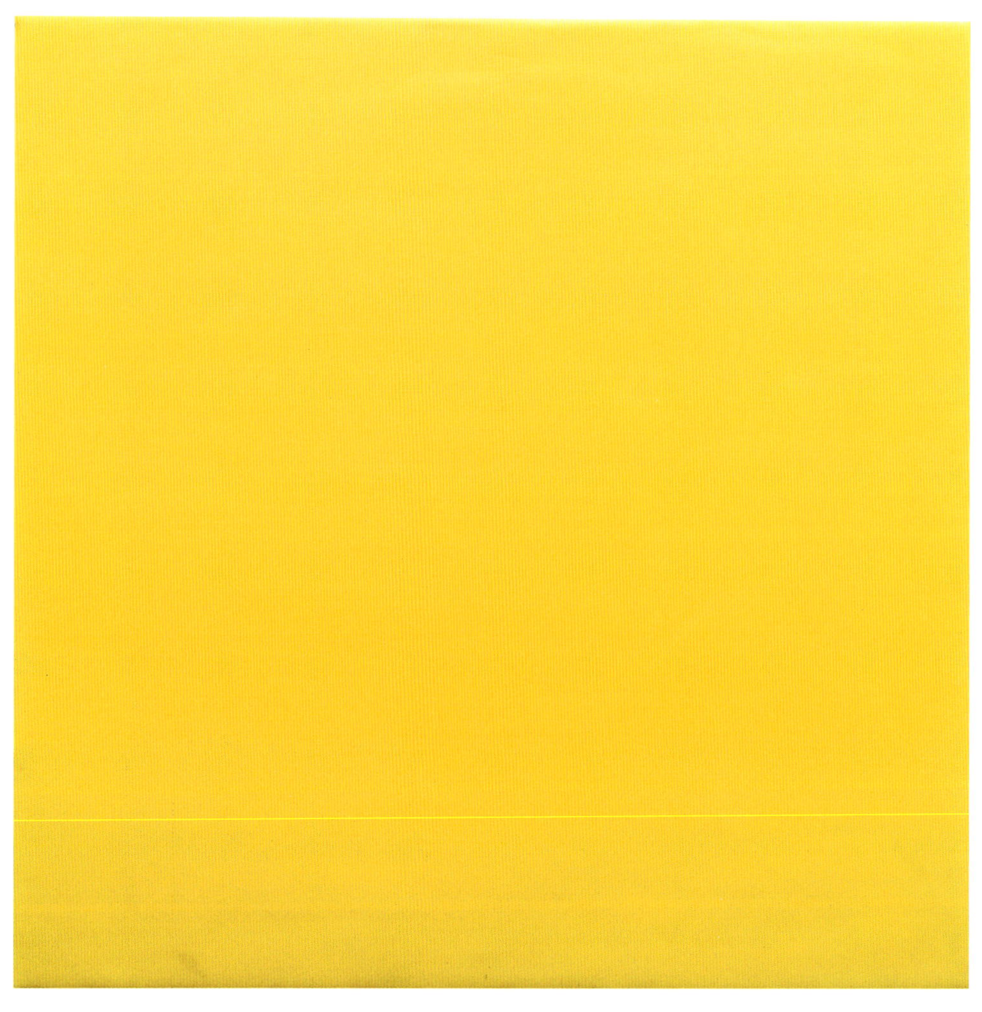

JOHN BEECH *Adhesive Painting*, 1996–2000
Glue on wood, 21 x 21 inches

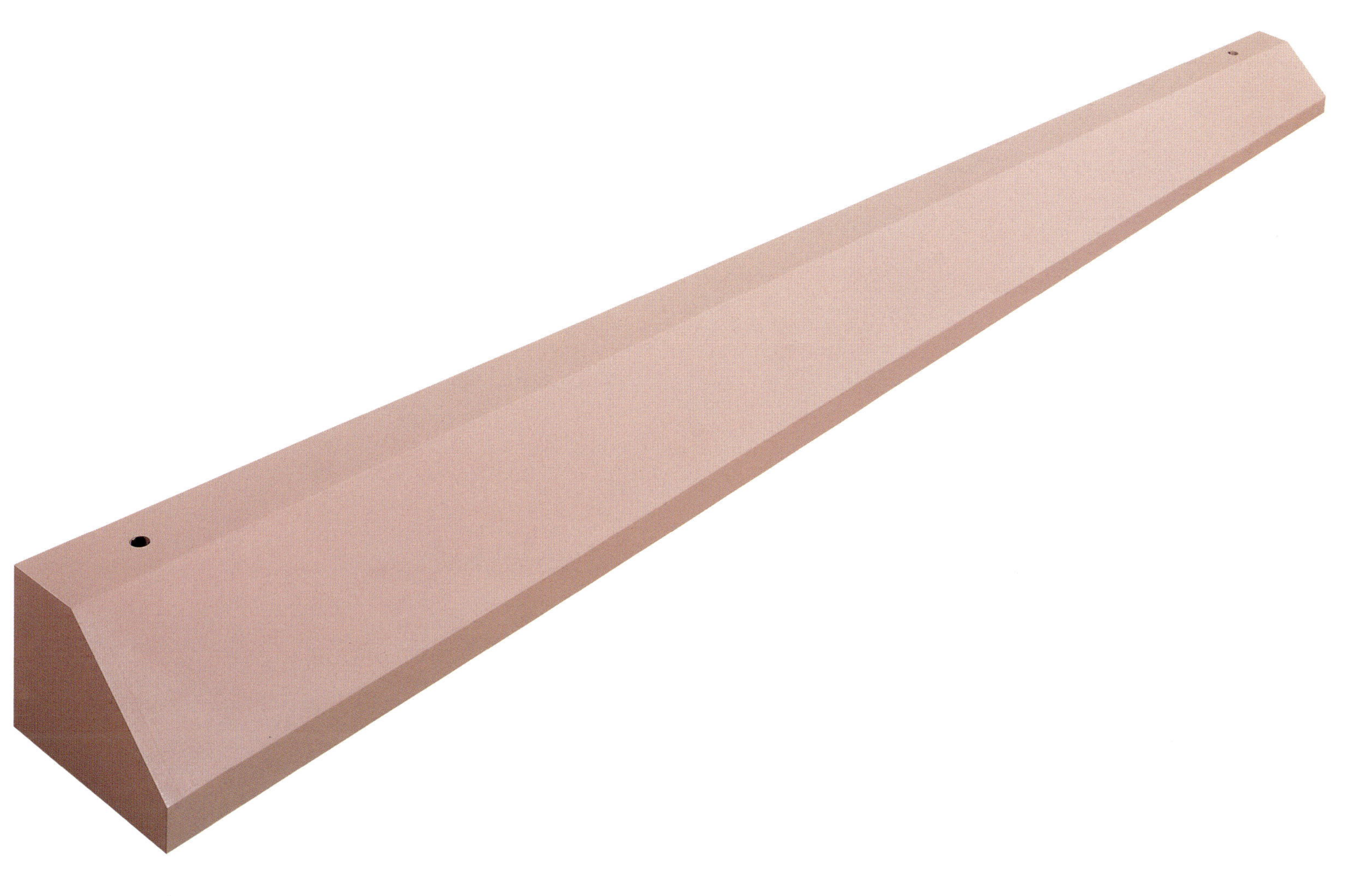

JOHN BEECH *Diminishing Bumper-Pink,* 2001
Enamel on wood and metal pipe, 8 x 98 x 11 inches

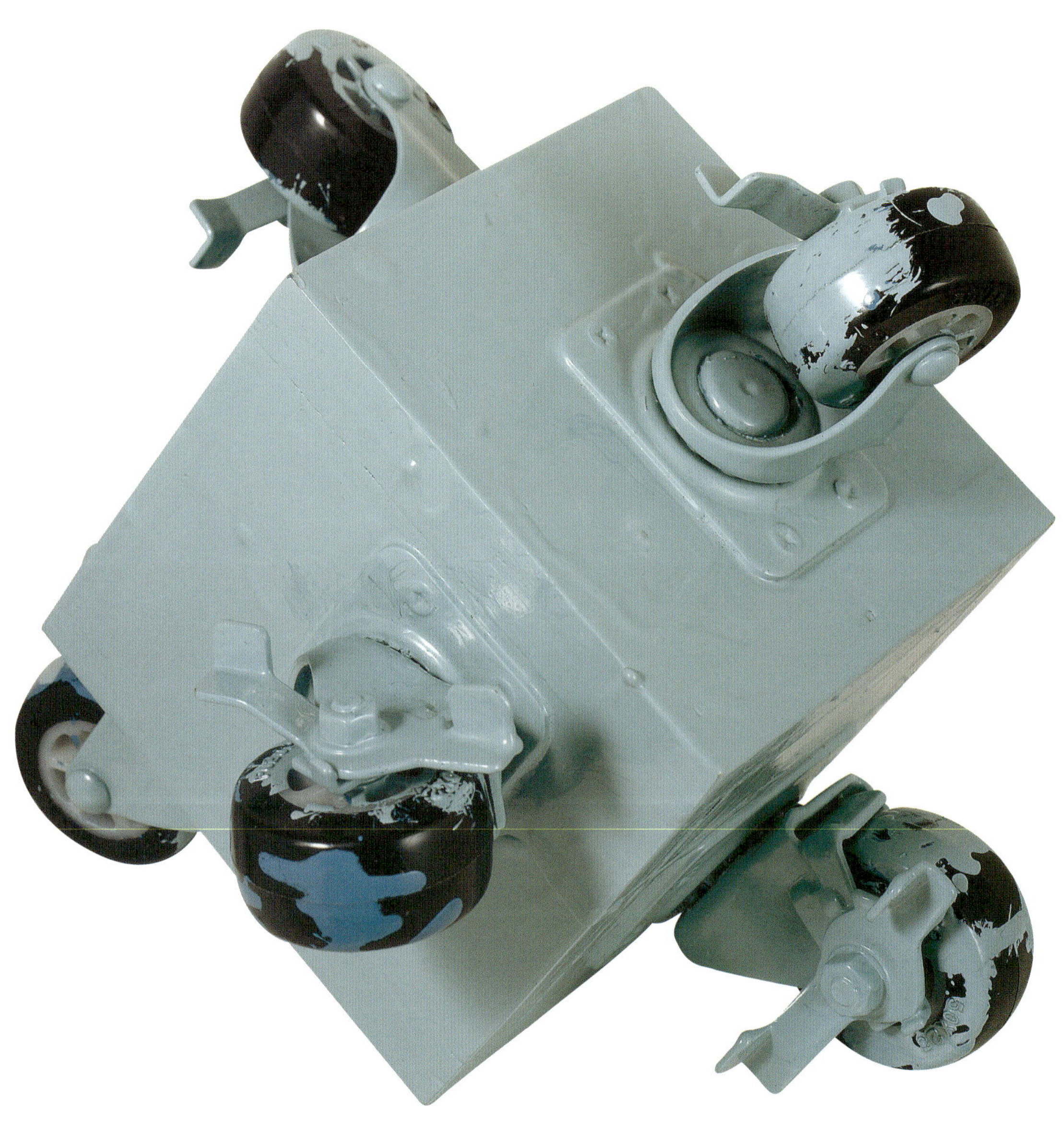

JOHN BEECH *Small Rolling Platform #49,* 2001
Enamel on wood and casters, 10 x 10 x 10 inches

JOHN BEECH *Bent Glue Painting,* 2002
Glue on canvas mounted on wood, 8 x 7½ x 9 inches

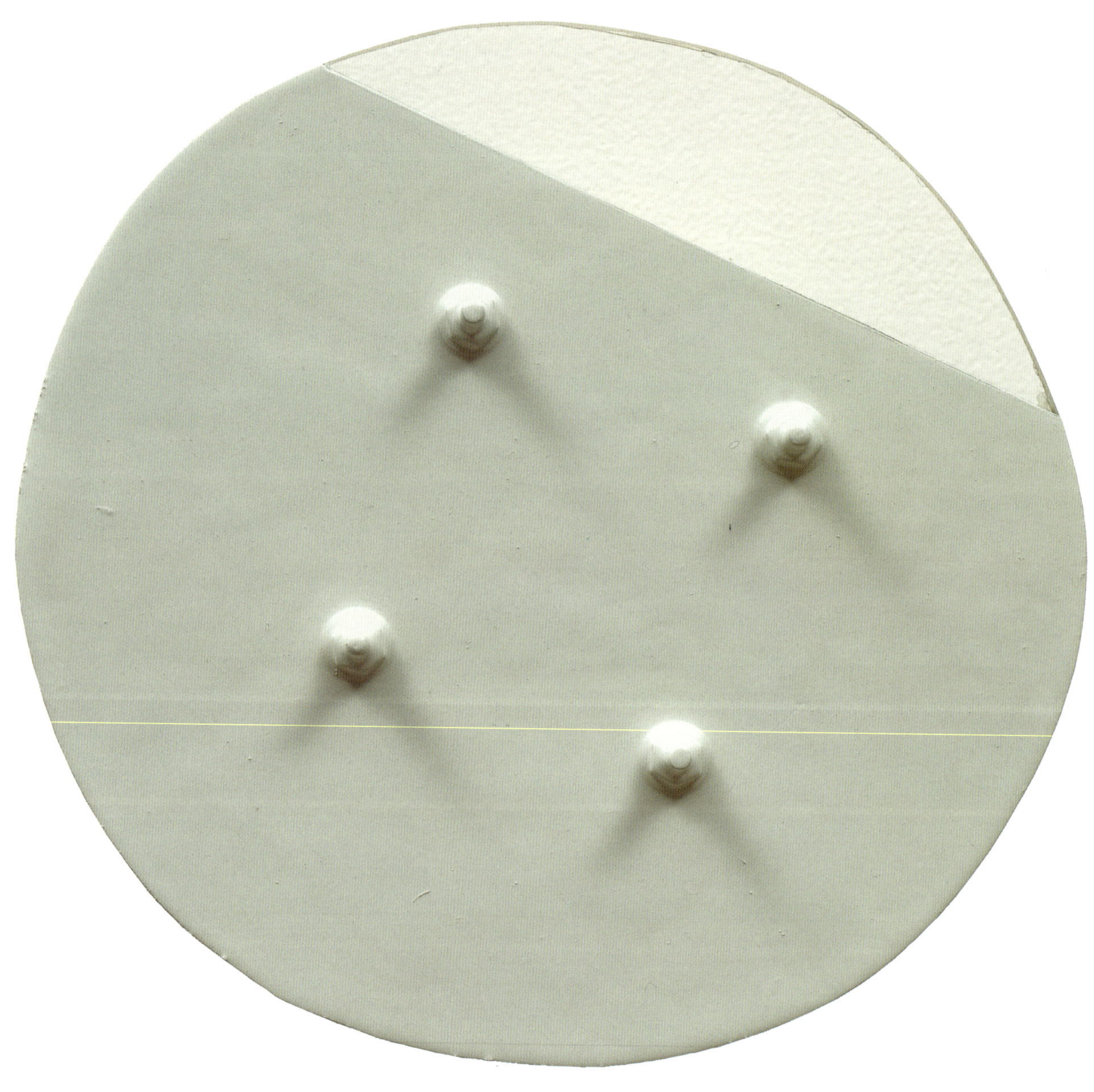

JOHN BEECH *Rotating Painting,* 2002
Enamel on Plexiglas mounted on wood, 8-inch diameter x 2½ inches

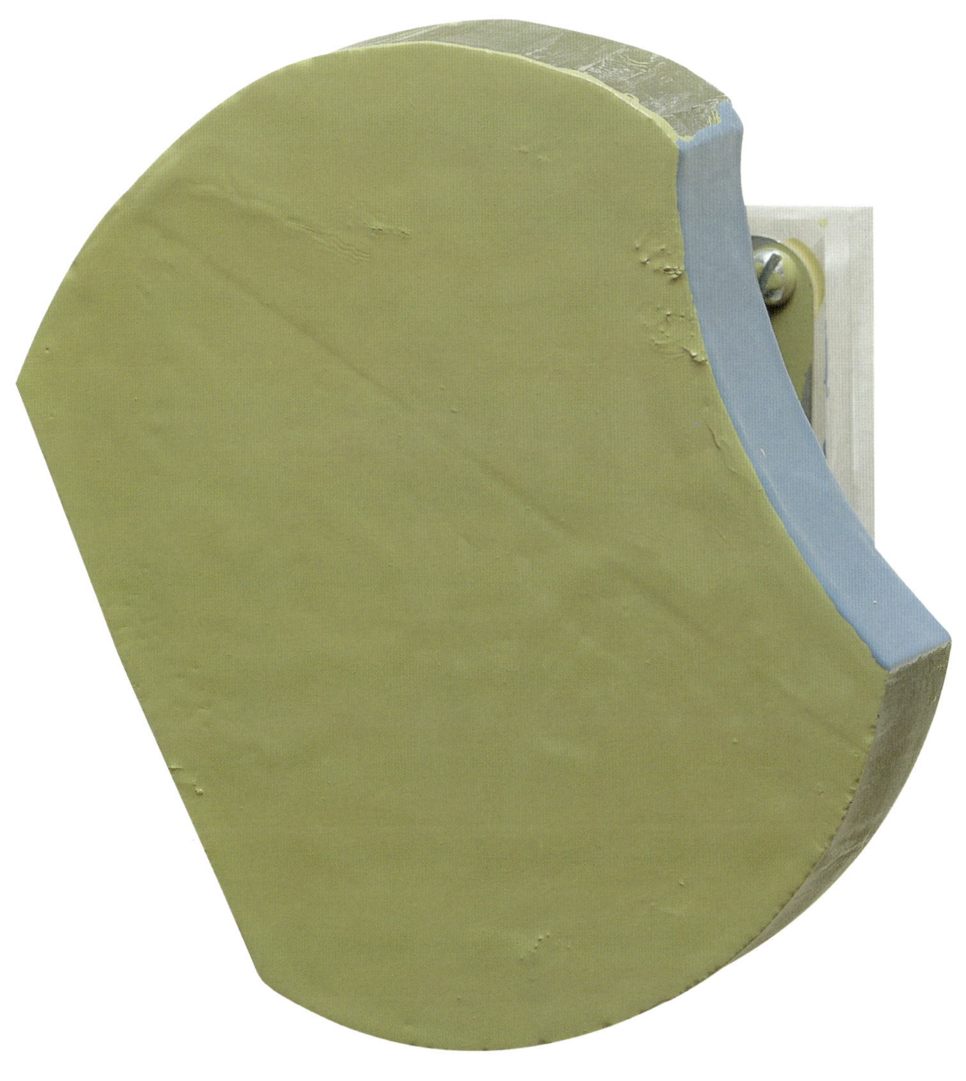

JOHN BEECH *RP #156*, 2003
Enamel on Plexiglas mounted on wood, 5 x 3⅝ x 2½ inches

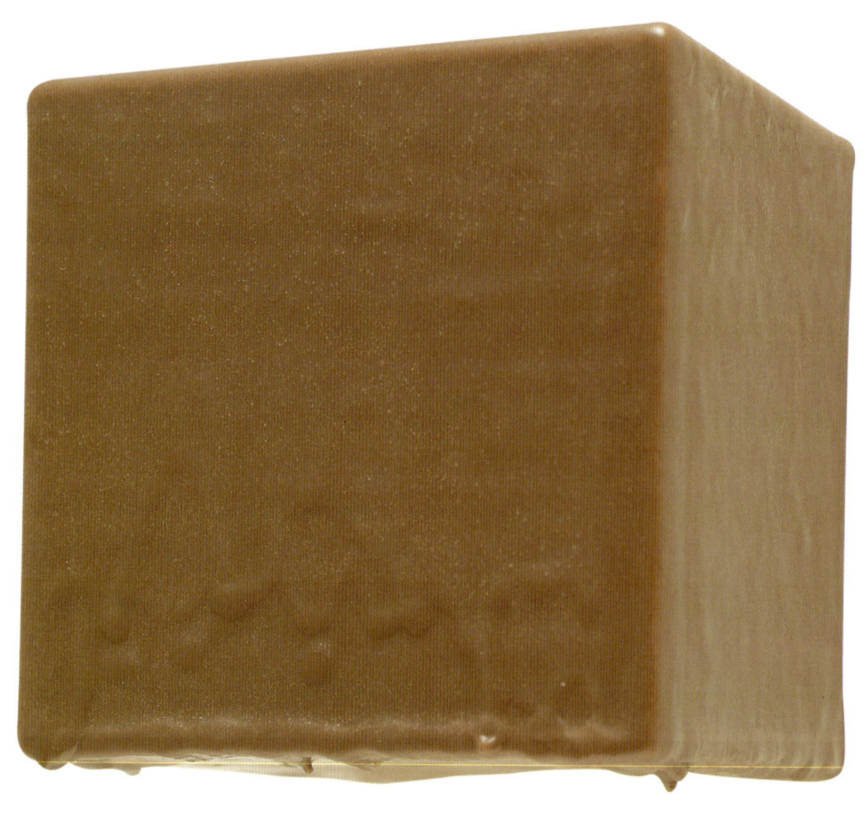

JOHN BEECH *Glue Painting #59,* 2004
Glue on wood, 4 x 4¾ x 4 inches

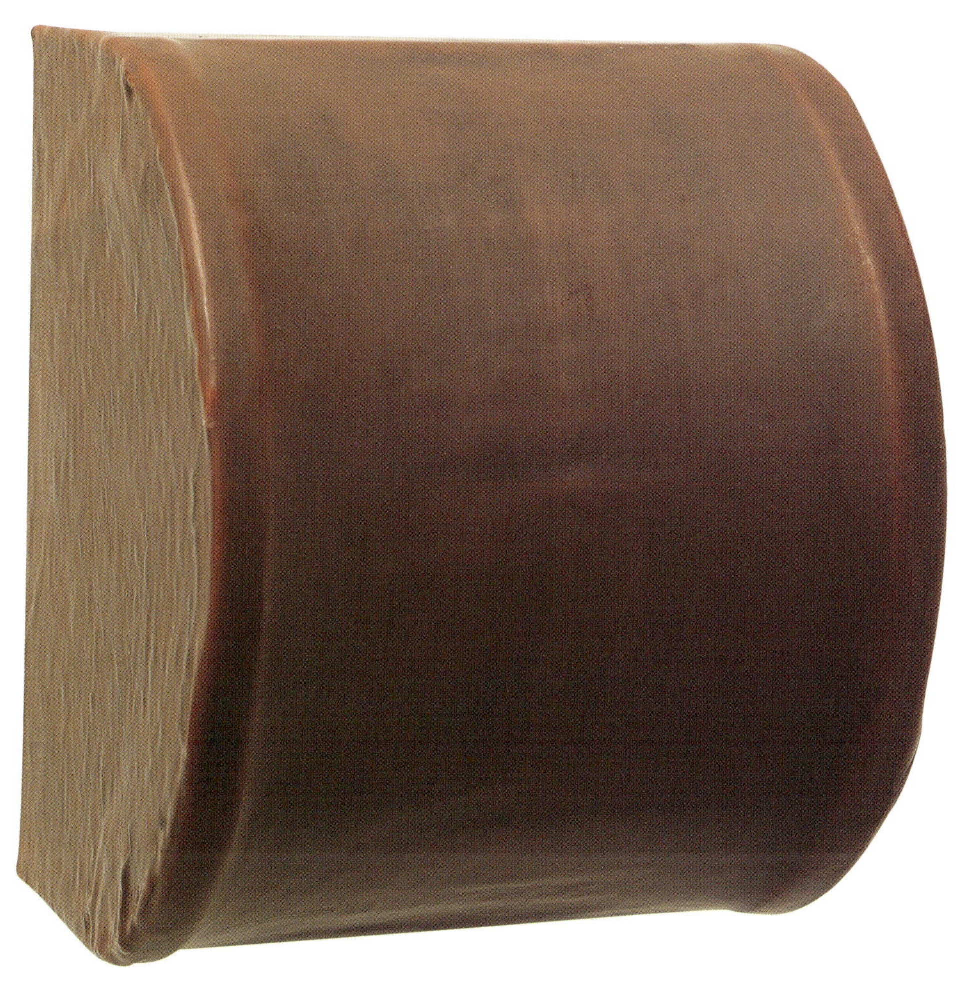

JOHN BEECH *Glue Painting #64,* 2004
Glue on wood, 9 ¾ x 7 ¾ x 7 ⅞ inches

TOM BENSON *Future,* 2000
Oil on aluminum, 23 5/8 x 24 1/4 inches

ERIKA BLUMENFELD *Aqua Blue/Light Green,* 2003
Automotive paint on Z-type aluminum, 19 ¼ x 23 ¼ inches

ERIKA BLUMENFELD *Untitled (Yellow/Light Gold),* 2003
Automotive paint on aluminum, Diptych, 7½ x 9½ inches each;
7½ x 19⅜ inches overall

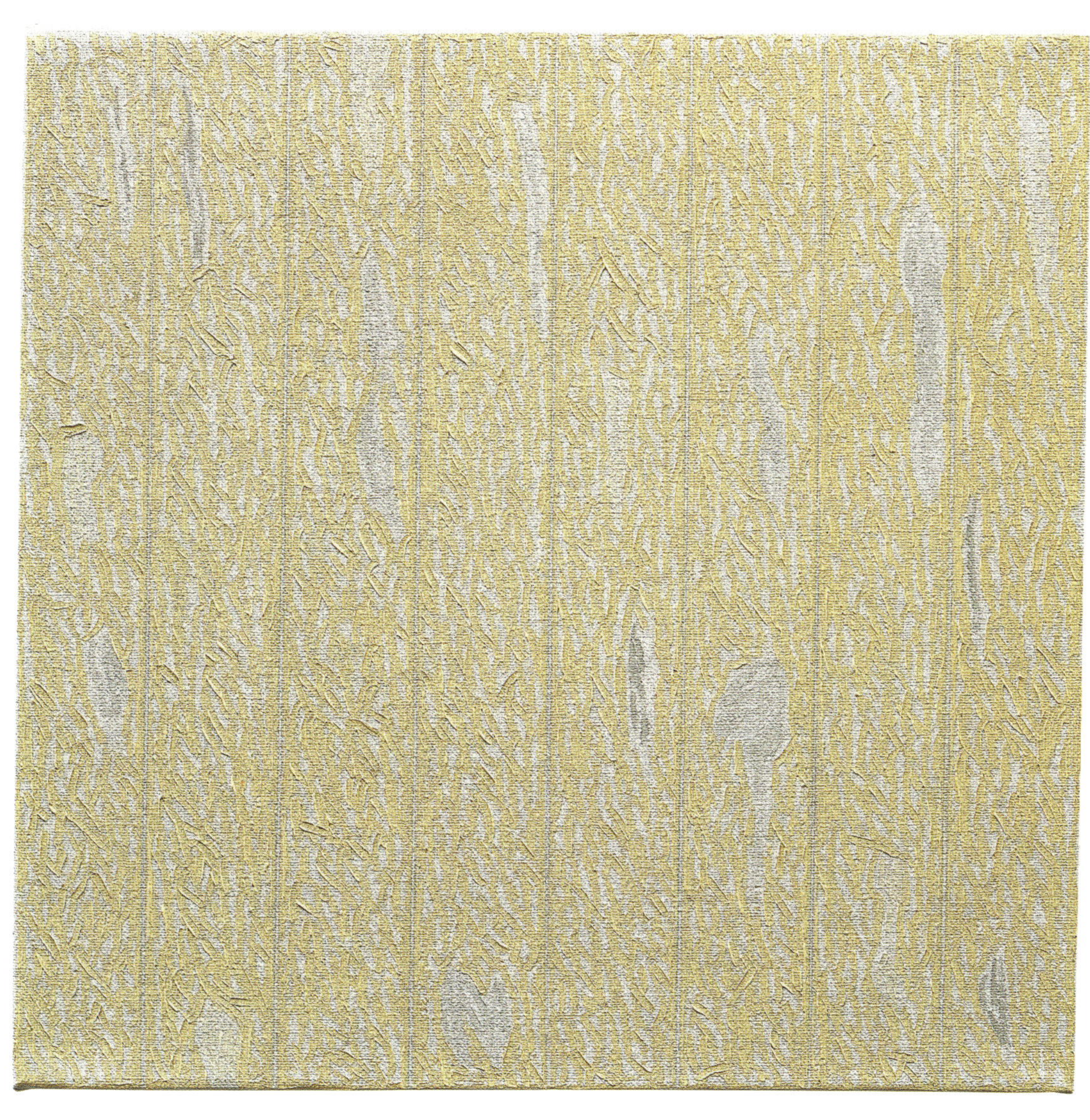

MALA BREUER *Not titled,* 1993
Oil on canvas, 12 x 12 inches

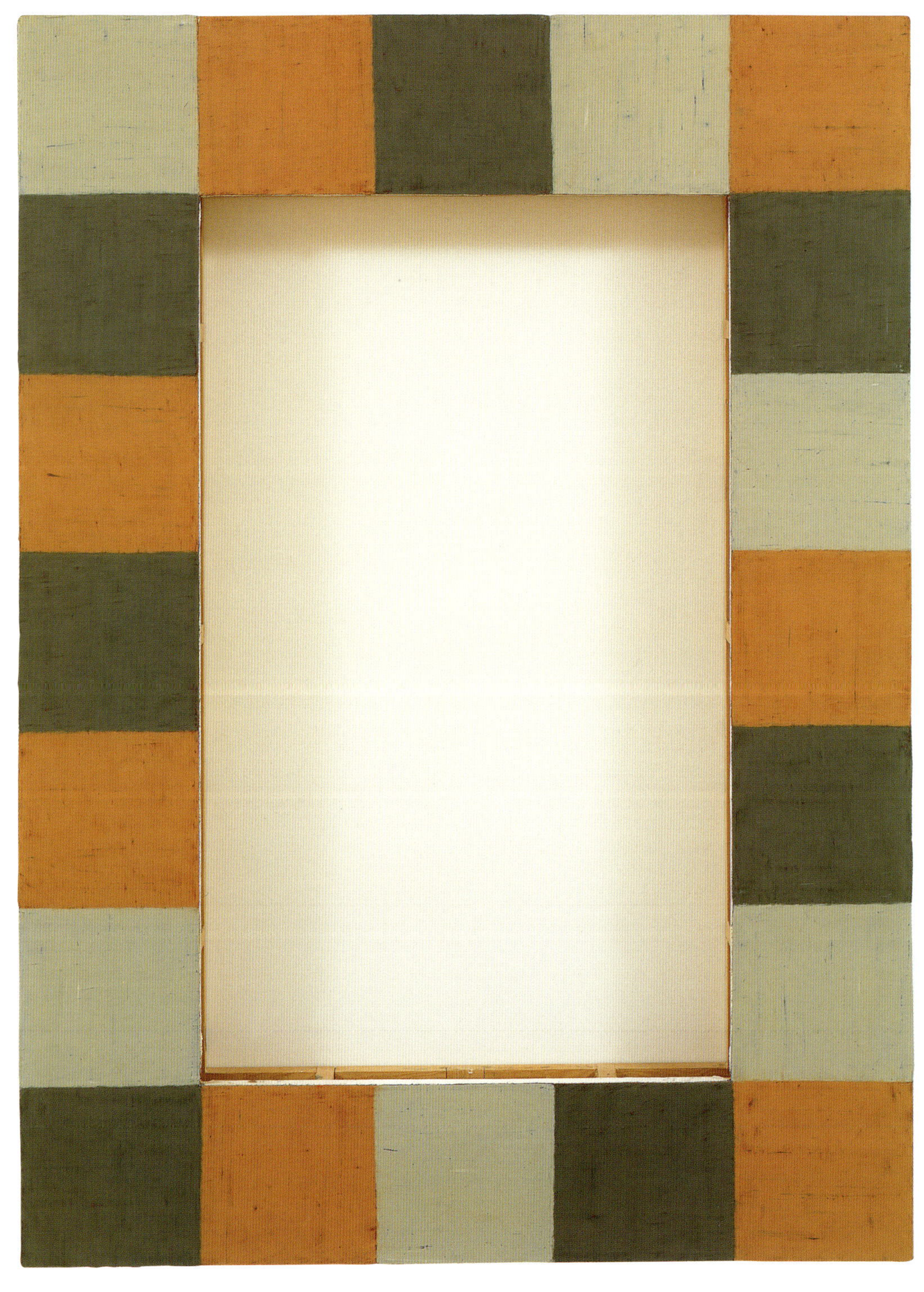

RODNEY CARSWELL *Two Grays and Orange Around an Empty Rectangle,* 1988
Oil and wax on canvas, 66 x 48 x 4 inches

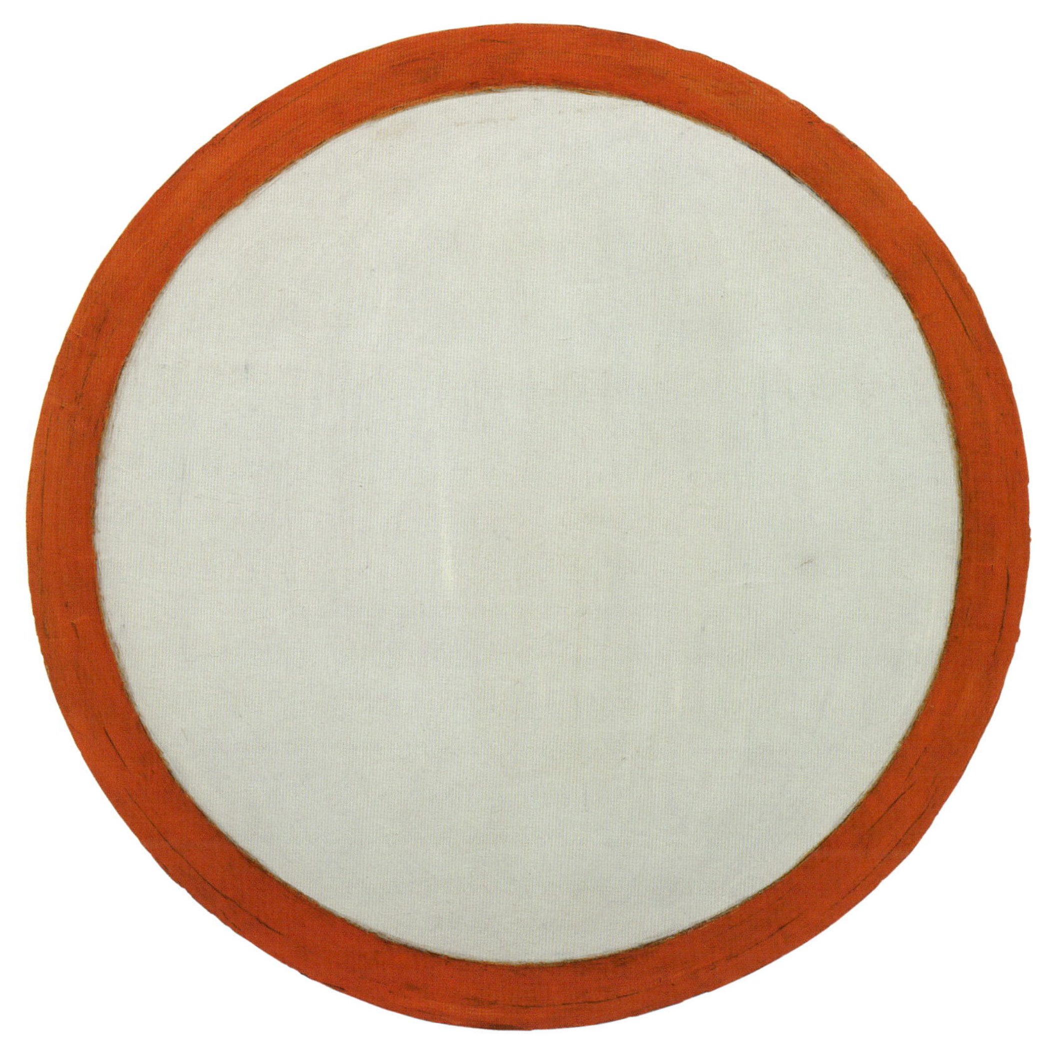

RODNEY CARSWELL *Red Circle / White Center,* 1991
Oil and wax on wood, 18 1/4-inch diameter x 3 1/4 inches

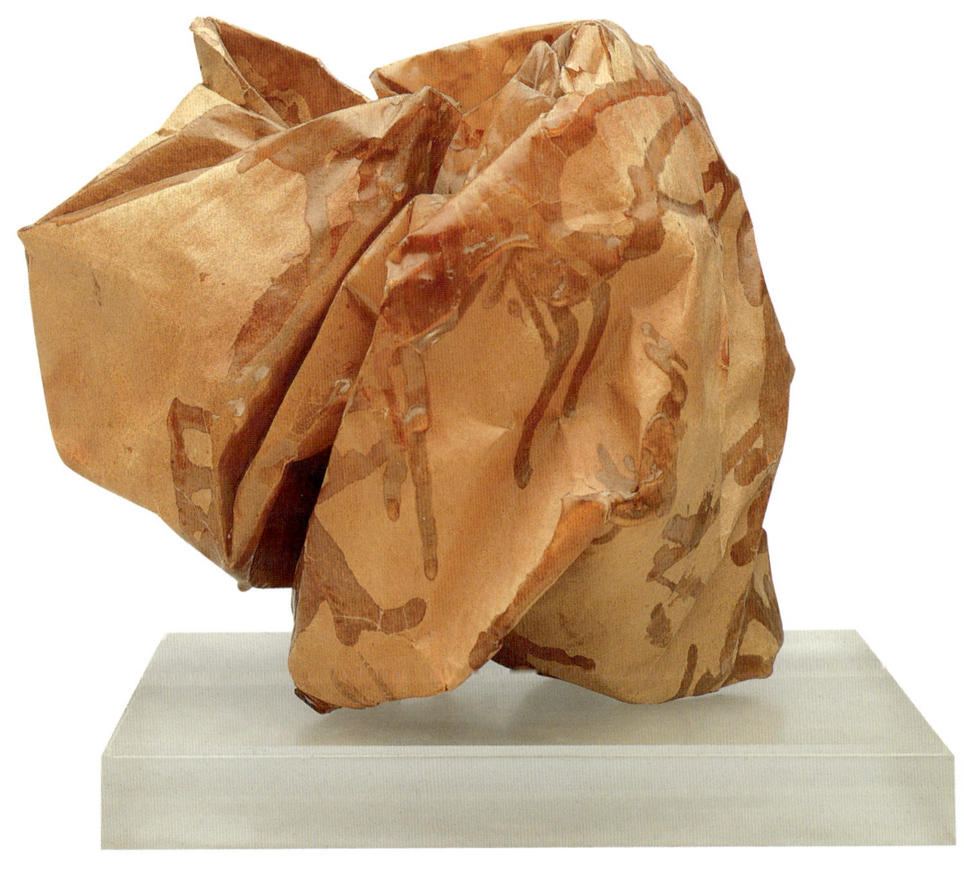

JOHN CHAMBERLAIN *Penthouse #69,* 1969
Paper bag, resin, and watercolor, 8 x 8 x 7 inches

MARK COLE *Not titled,* 2002
Polyurethane cast, 28 x 30 inches

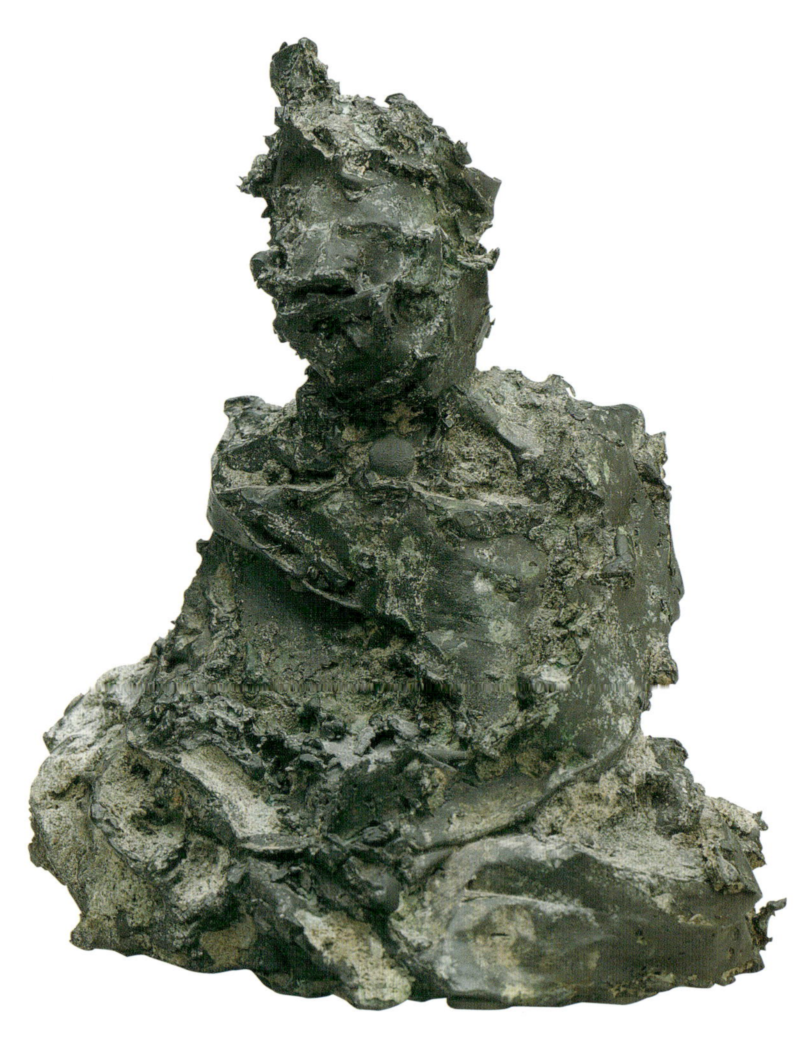

JOHN CONNELL *Not titled,* CA. 1985
Bronze, 10 x 6 x 4 inches

RUDOLF DE CRIGNIS *Painting #96.9,* 1996
Oil on canvas, 30 x 30 inches

RUDOLF DE CRIGNIS *Painting #98.7,* 1998
Oil on canvas, 60 x 60 inches

RUDOLF DE CRIGNIS *Painting #01-37*, 2001
Oil on canvas, 60 x 60 inches

CONSTANCE DEJONG *Square IV,* 1992
Paint on copper, 36 x 36 inches

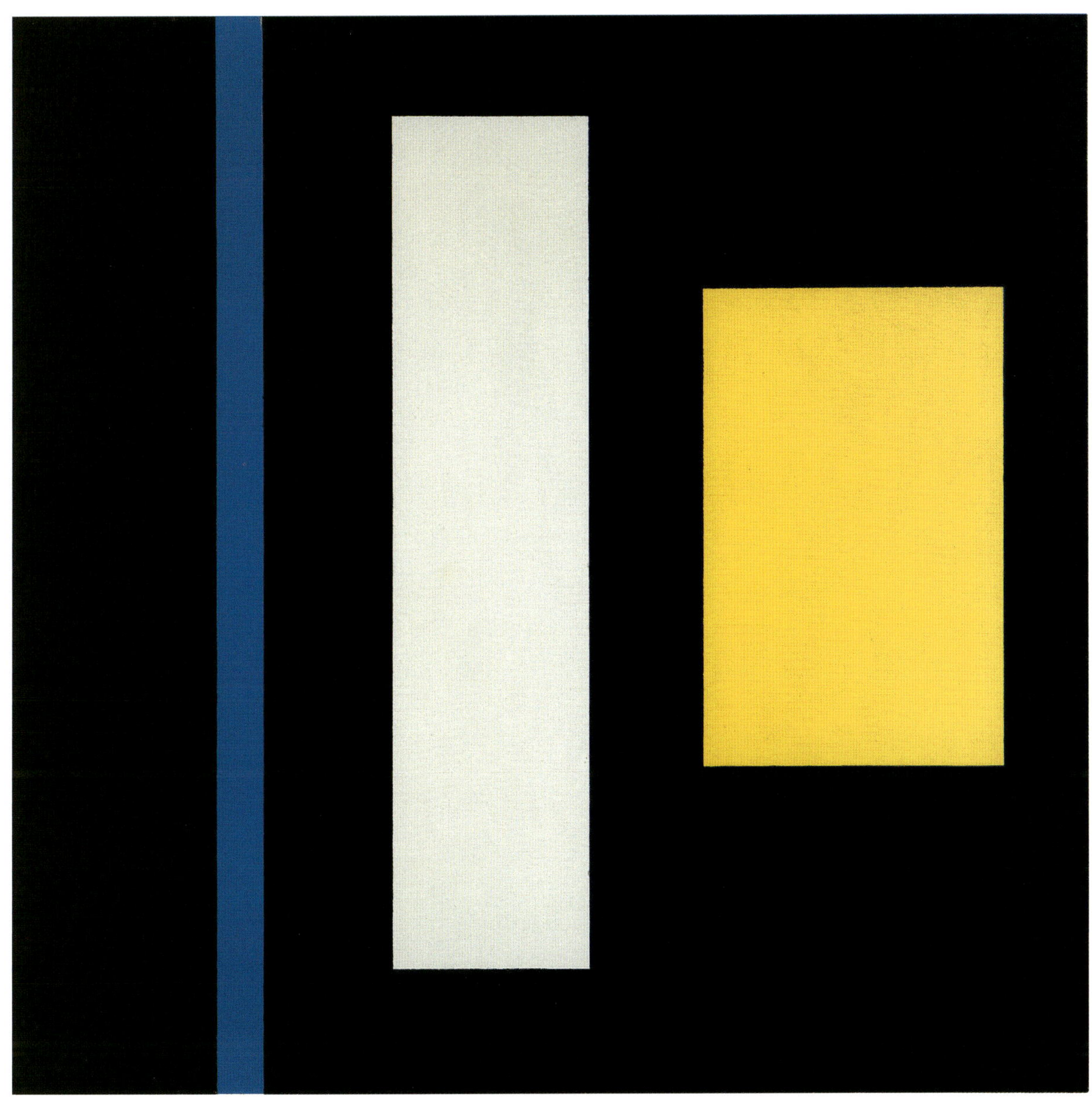

BURGOYNE DILLER *First Theme #35,* 1955–1960
Oil on canvas, 42 x 42 inches

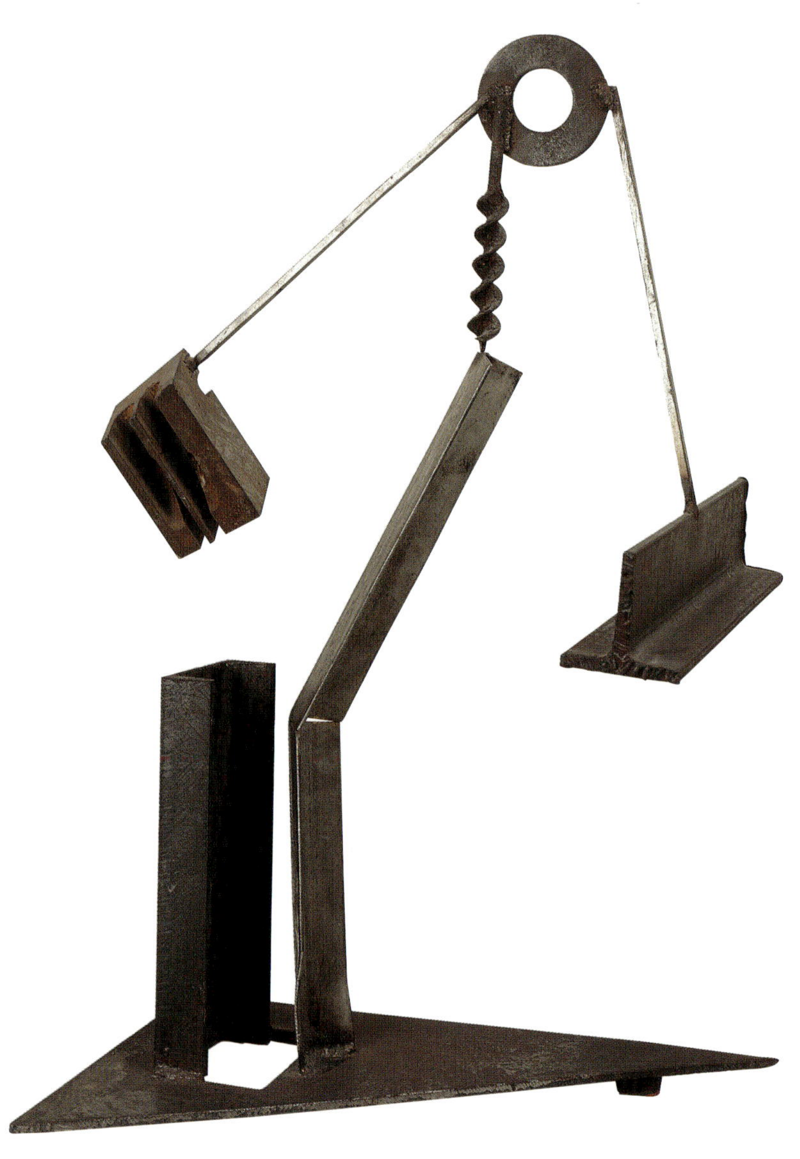

MARK DI SUVERO *Untitled,* 1967
Steel, 29 ¼ x 26 x 17 inches

ALAN EBNOTHER *Abomination,* 1996
Oil on linen, 62 x 59 inches

ALAN EBNOTHER *Accord,* 1997
Oil on copper mounted on wood, 12 ¾ x 10 ¼ inches

ALAN EBNOTHER *Angry,* 2000
Oil on linen, 59 x 57 inches

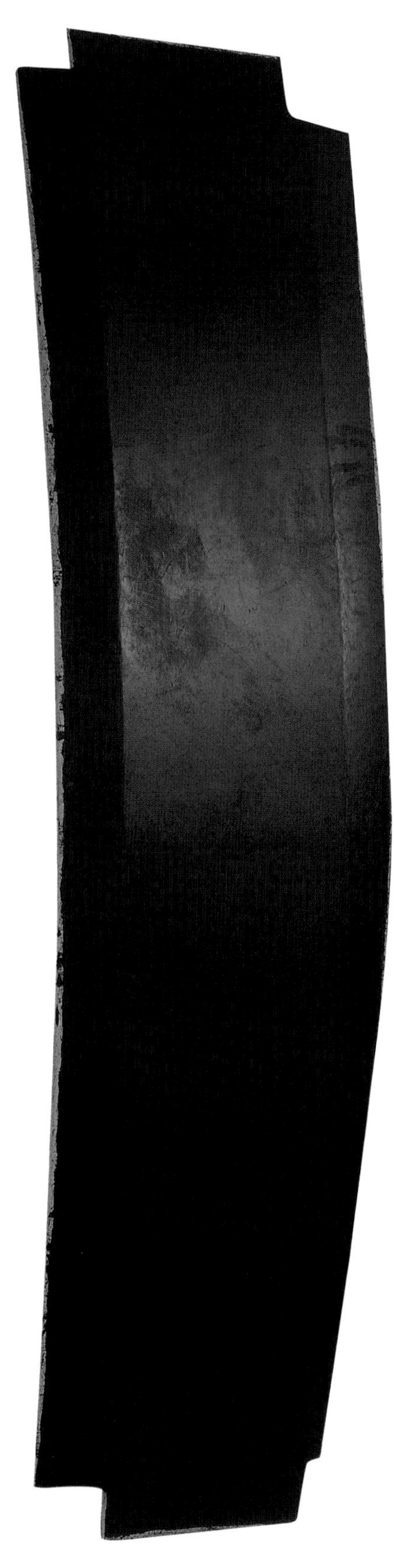

ALLAN GRAHAM *Hinge*, 1987
Oil and wax on linen, 96 x 27 x 6½ inches

GLORIA GRAHAM *FeS2 Pyrite,* 1997
Watercolor and kaolin with wax on cotton mounted on wood, 14 x 14 inches

MARCIA HAFIF *Roman Painting XXVII,* 1988
Oil over acrylic on linen, 13 x 12 inches

MARCIA HAFIF *French Painting: Terraile,* 1990
Oil on cotton, 60 x 60 inches

MARCIA HAFIF *Red Painting: Indian Yellow Tint,* 1998
Oil on cotton, 58 x 58 inches

MARCIA HAFIF *Red Painting: Paliogen Maroon,* 1998
Oil on cotton, 58 x 58 inches

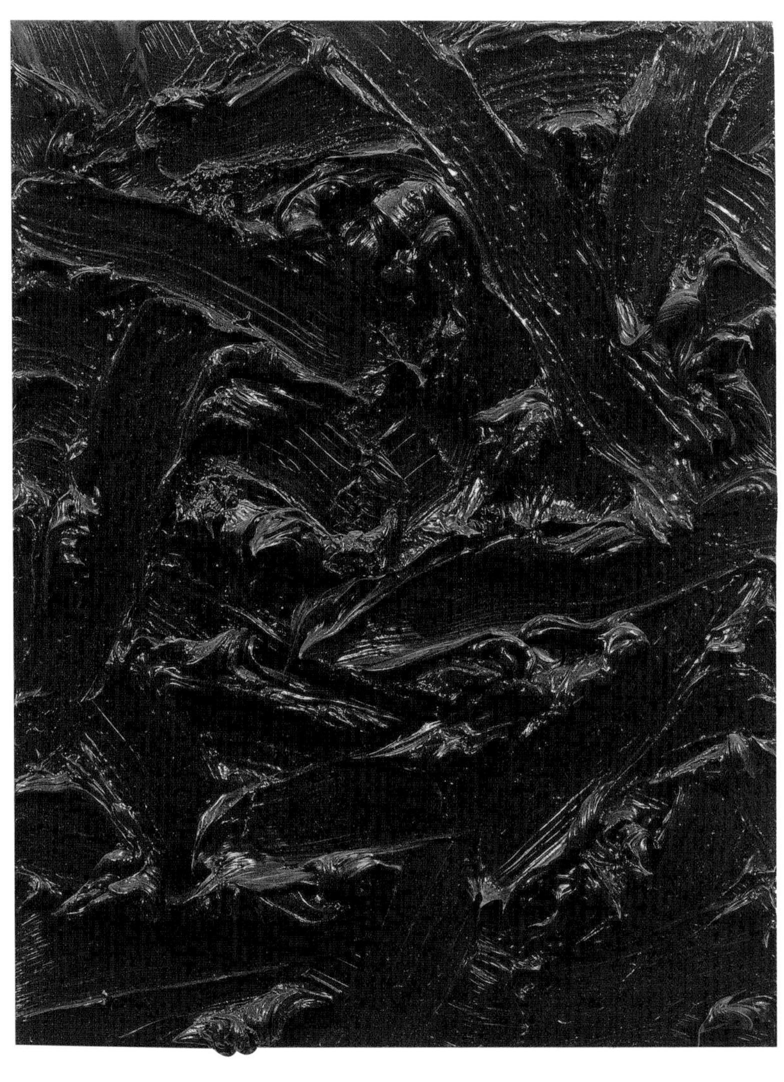

JAMES HAYWARD *Chromachord #49,* 1999
Oil on canvas mounted on board, 13½ x 10½ inches

JAMES HOWELL *Clay Series No. 1* and *Clay Series No. 2* (units 1 & 2 of 9), 1992
Acrylic on aluminum, Diptych, 18 x 18 inches each; 18 x 38 inches overall

JAMES HOWELL *Light Stone Veil,* 1992
Acrylic on aluminum, 48 x 48 inches

JAMES HOWELL *San Juan Series No. 6* and *San Juan Series No. 7* (units 6 & 7 of 10), 1993
Acrylic on aluminum, Diptych, 18 x 18 inches each; 18 x 38 inches overall

JAMES HOWELL *(S6.4) Set 93.02,* 1995
Acrylic on cotton duck, 60 x 60 inches

JAMES HOWELL *Dark Suite Four Part Painting,* 2000-2001,
Acrylic on canvas, 15½ x 15½ inches each; 15½ x 92 inches overall

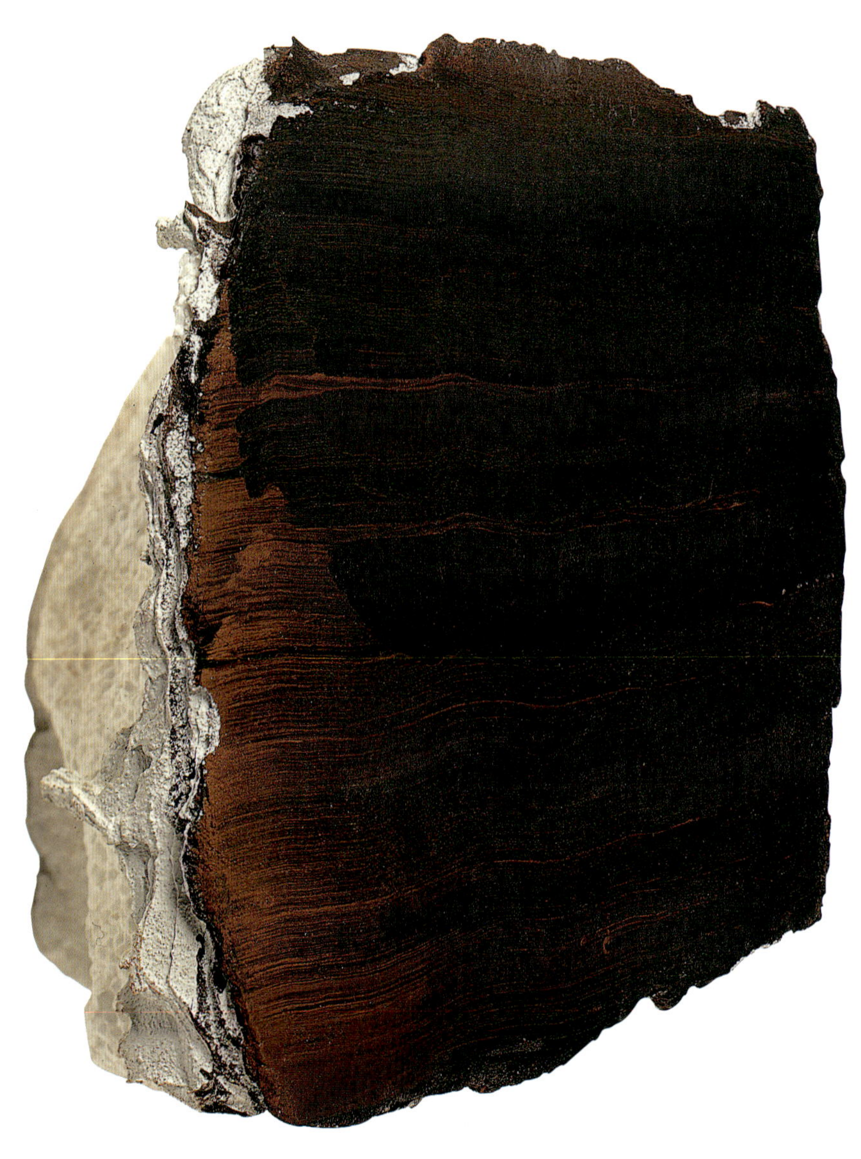

JAMES HYDE *Part,* 1993
Fresco on Styrofoam, 9 ¼ x 10 x 5 inches

RACHEL LACHOWICZ *Not titled,* 2003
Lipstick on canvas, 26 x 20 inches

JODY LOMBERG *Slip 11,* 1993
Mixed media on canvas, 36 x 50 inches

ED MALINA *103B*, 1991
Acrylic on wood, 19 x 23 inches

ED MALINA *103W*, 1991
Acrylic on wood, 19 x 20 inches

ED MALINA *242B*, 1992
Acrylic on wood, 20 x 20 inches

JOSEPH MARIONI *Red Painting*, 1995
Acrylic on linen, 79 x 76 inches

JOSEPH MARIONI *Green Painting,* 1996
Acrylic on linen, 71½ x 68 inches

JOSEPH MARIONI *White Painting*, 1997
Acrylic on linen, 55 x 51 inches

JOSEPH MARIONI *Yellow Painting,* 1997
Acrylic on linen, 79 x 74 inches

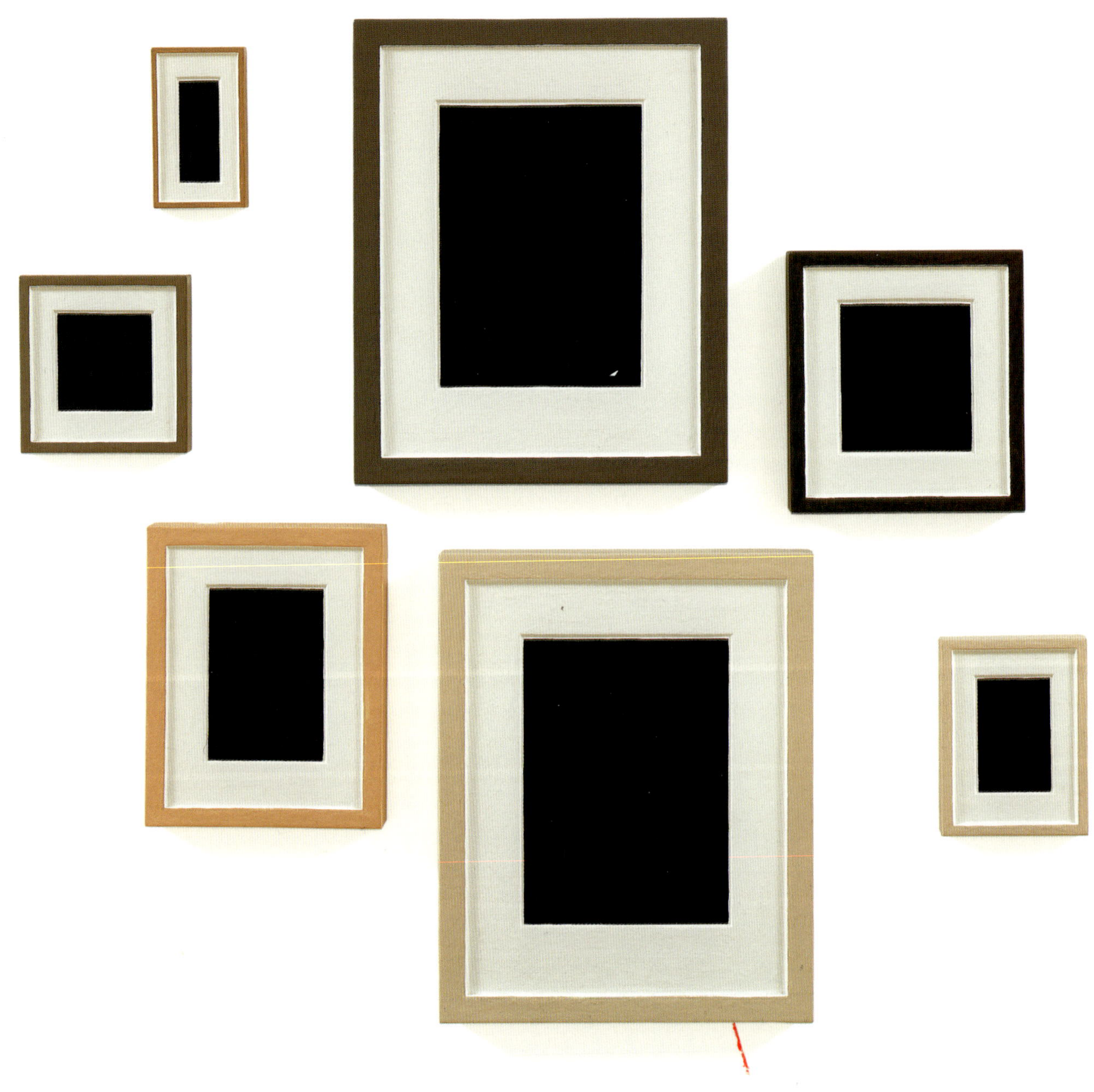

ALLAN MCCOLLUM *Surrogates Paintings,* 1983
Acrylic on plaster, CLOCKWISE: *#19-1-1983*, 20 x 16 in.; *#4-10-1983*, 11 ¾ x 10 in.; *#8-15-1983*, 8 ½ x 6 ¼ in.; *#8-1-1983*, 20 x 16 in.; *#5-7-1983*, 13 x 10 in.; *#21-16-1983*, 7 ¾ x 7 ¼ in.; *#7-17-1983*, 7 x 4 in.

JOHN MEYER *Not titled, ca.* 1989
Oil on linen, 65 x 64½ inches

JOHN MEYER *Not titled,* 1991
Oil on linen, 36 x 36 inches

JOHN MEYER *Not titled,* 1993-1995
Egg tempera, gesso, and linen mounted on oak panel, Diptych,
72 x 72 x 5 inches each; 72 x 148 x 5 inches overall

JOHN MEYER *Not titled,* 1994
Tempera on mahogany panel, Diptych, 18½ x 18½ inches each; 18½ x 37 inches overall

JOHN MEYER *Not titled,* 1996
Egg tempera on walnut panel, Diptych, 20 x 20 inches each;
20 x 41 inches overall

JOHN MEYER *Not titled,* 1997
Egg tempera on wood, Diptych, 24 x 24 inches each;
24 x 49 inches overall

JOHN MEYER *Not titled,* 2000
Ground lapis and ground malachite with egg tempera on white oak panel, Diptych, 10 x 10 inches each; 10 x 20 inches overall

JOHN MEYER *Not titled,* 2001
Tempera on walnut panel, 17 x 19 inches

PATRICIA MOISAN *Perforation,* 1995
Pigment and resin on aluminum, 20 x 20 inches

DOUG OHLSON *Sneaky-Pete,* 1965–1966
Oil on canvas, Joined diptych, 24 x 48 inches

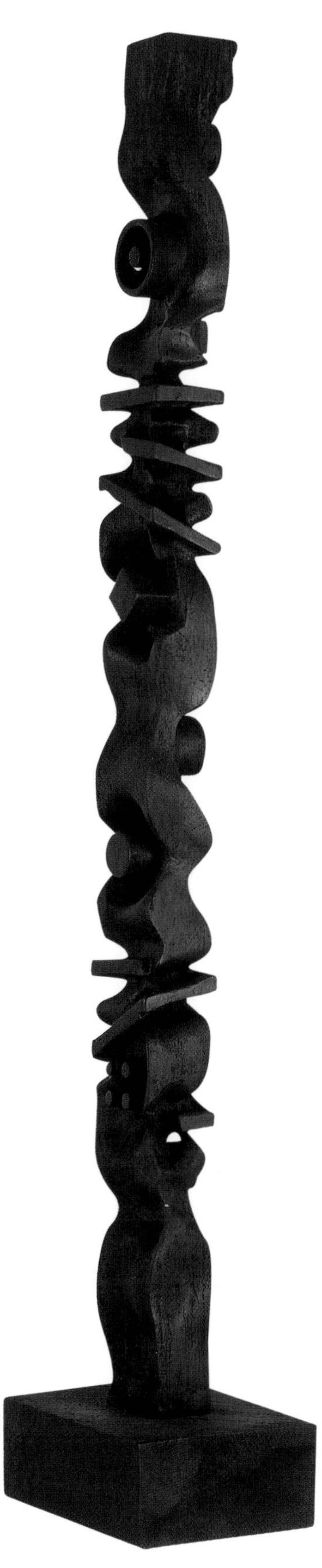

FLORENCE PIERCE *Totem #6,* 1967
Oil pigment on wood, 52 x 7½ x 9½ inches

FLORENCE PIERCE *Untitled #9,* 1994
Resin relief on mirrored Plexiglas, 24 x 24 inches

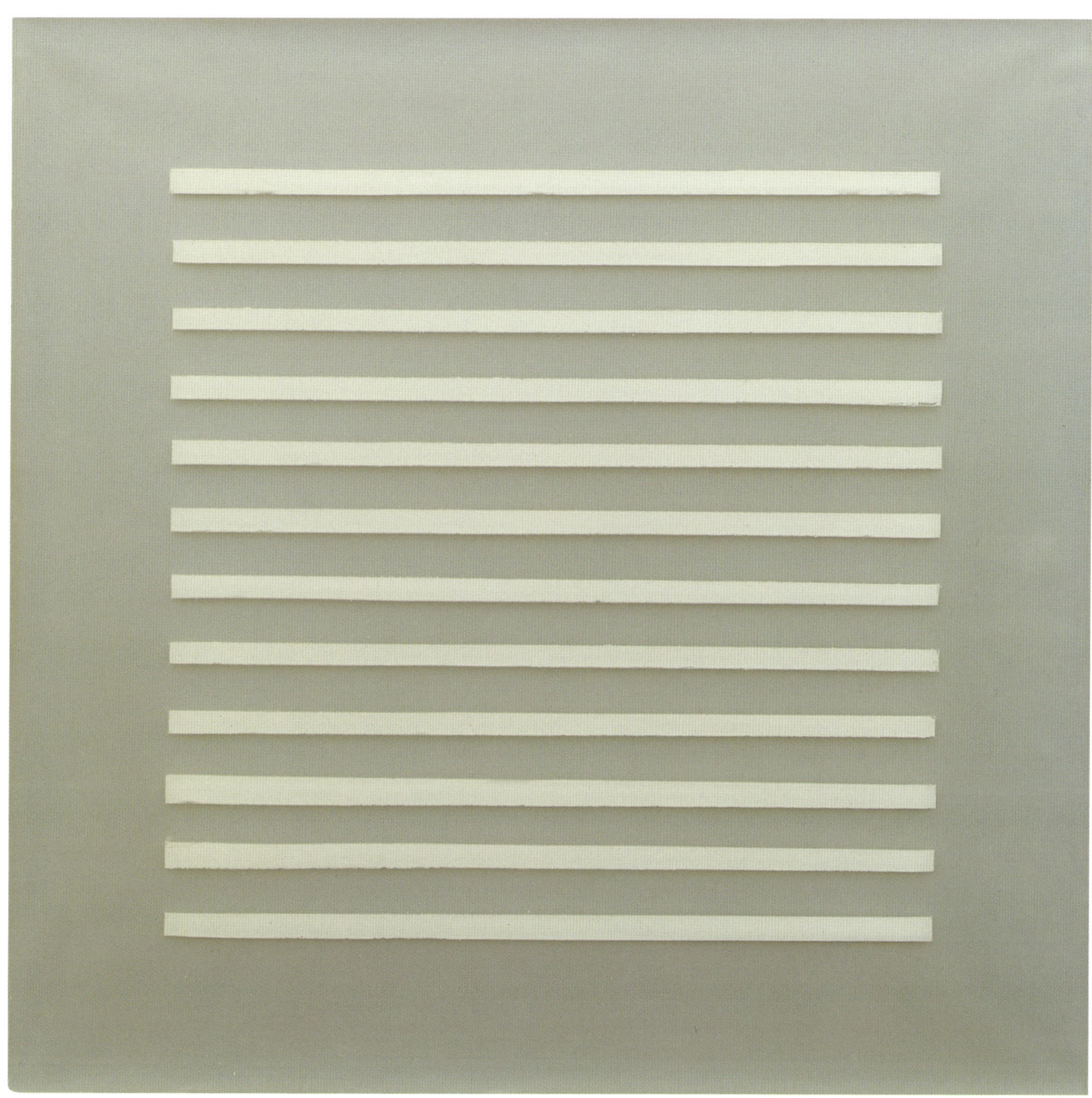

FLORENCE PIERCE *Untitled #16*, 1994
Resin relief on mirrored Plexiglas, 24 x 24 inches

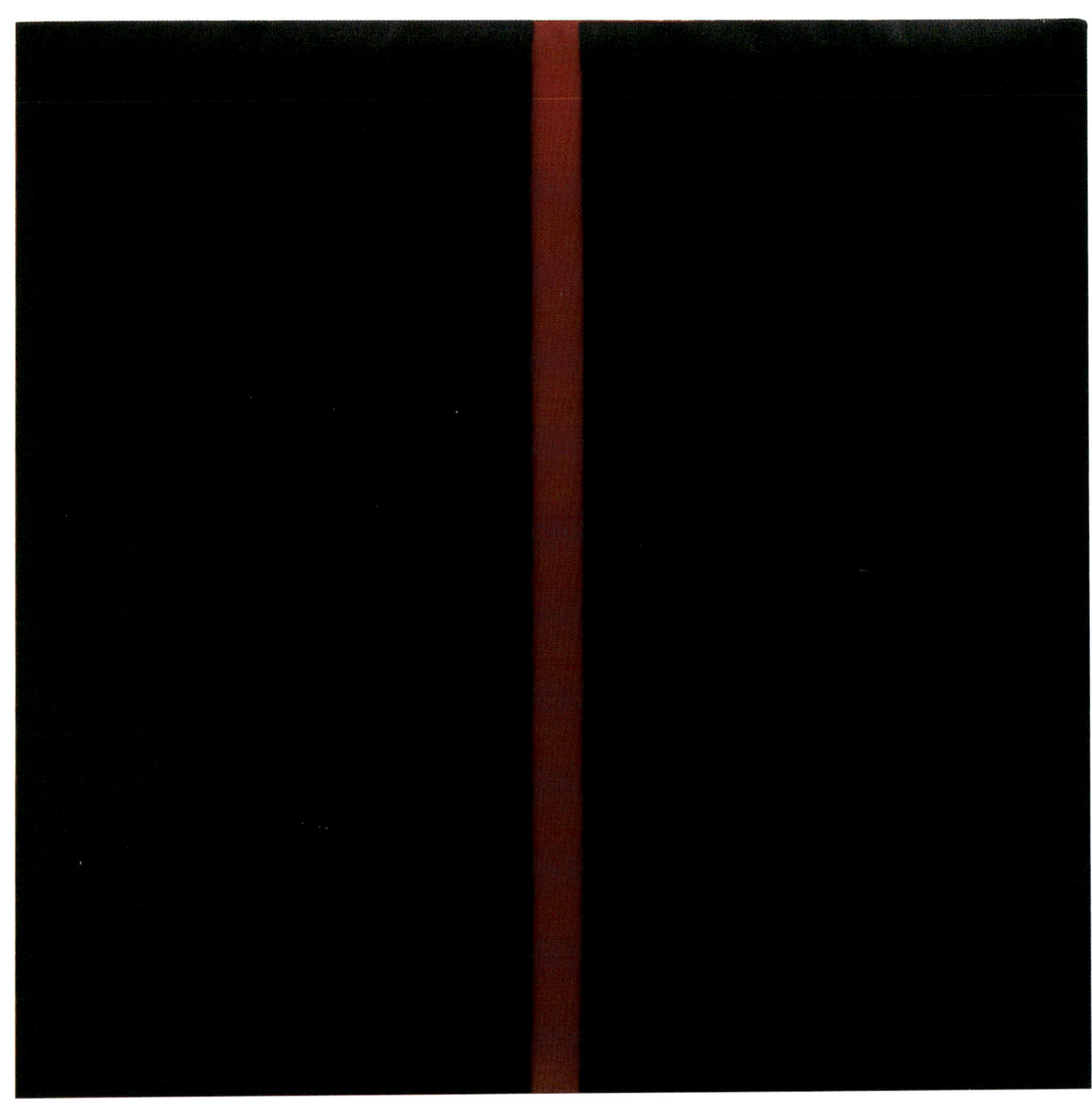

FLORENCE PIERCE *Untitled #117*, 1995
Resin relief on mirrored Plexiglas, 24 x 24 inches

FLORENCE PIERCE *Untitled #246 (Pink)*, 1999
Resin relief on mirrored Plexiglas, 24 x 24 inches

FLORENCE PIERCE *Untitled #346,* 1999
Resin relief on mirrored Plexiglas, 24 x 24 inches

FLORENCE PIERCE *Untitled #598,* 2002
Resin relief on mirrored Plexiglas, 24 x 24 inches

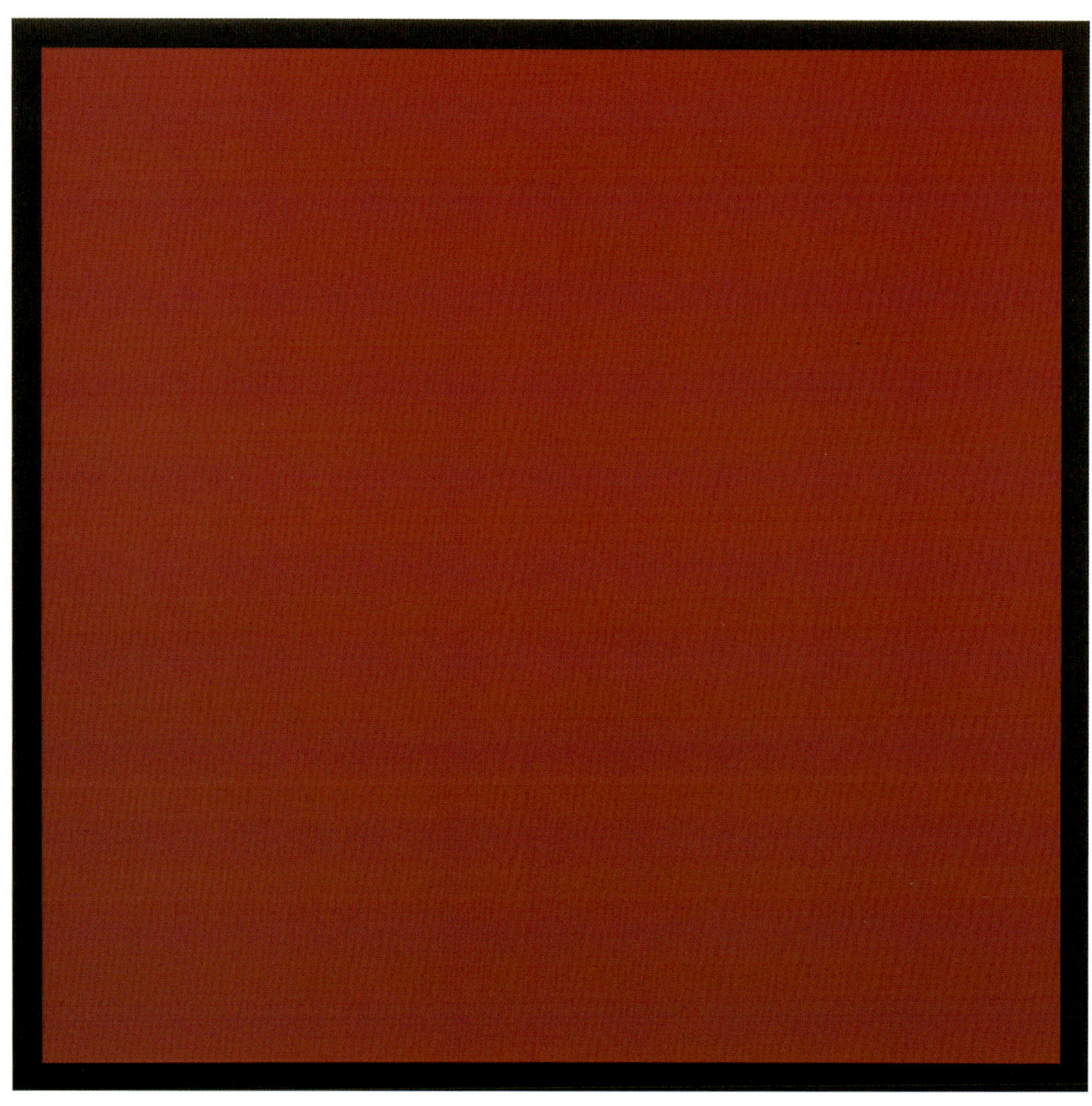

WINSTON ROETH *Luzerne,* 1994
Tempera on fiberboard, 32 x 32 inches

WINSTON ROETH *Dark 3x4*, 1995
Tempera on cotton duck mounted on panel, 48 x 36 inches

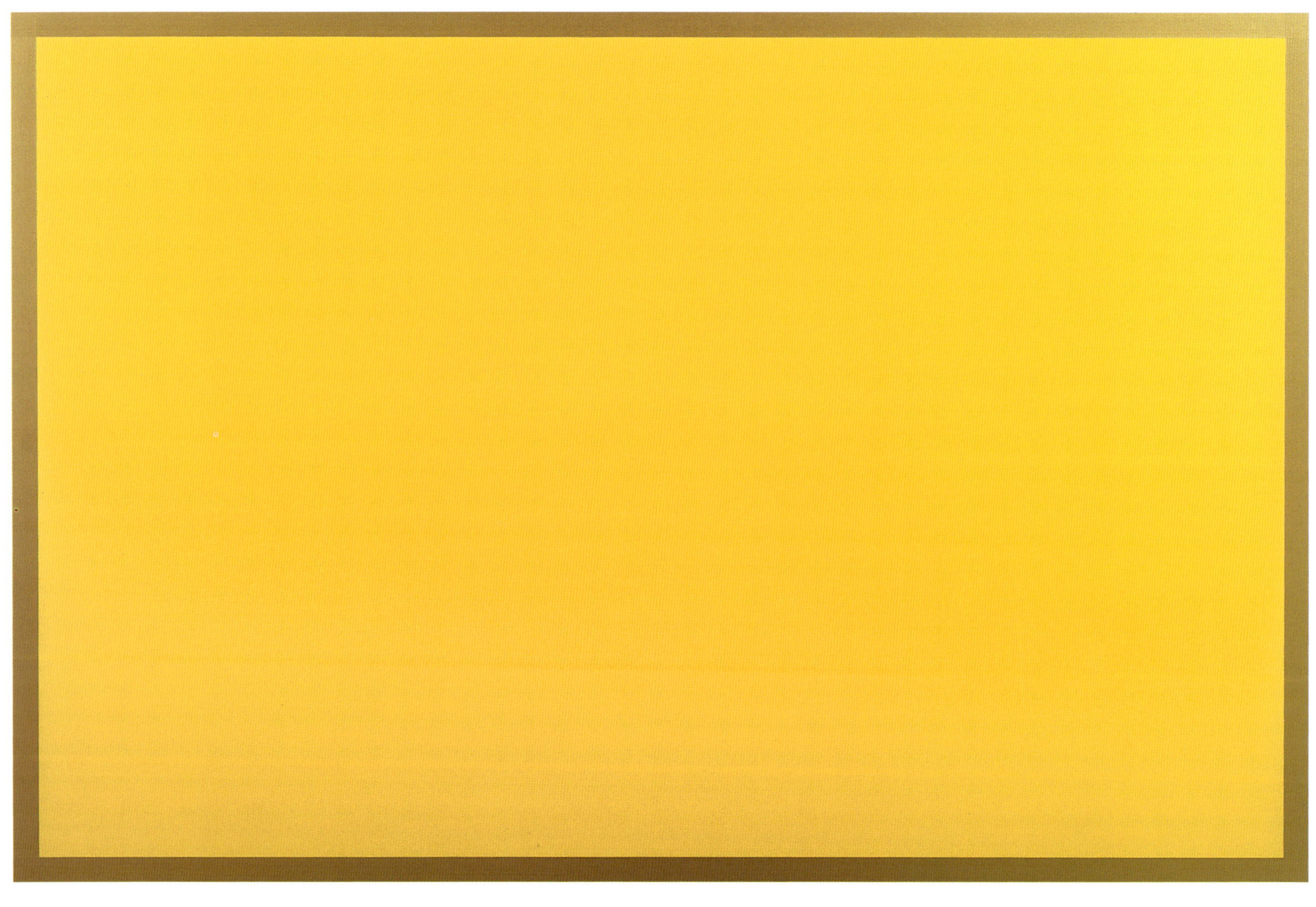

WINSTON ROETH *Dreamer*, 2002
Tempera on panel, 54 x 80 inches

MICHAEL ROUILLARD *Not titled*, 1994
Acrylic on Plexiglas, 48 x 30 inches

MICHAEL ROUILLARD *Not titled,* 1994
Acrylic on Plexiglas, 44½ x 28 inches

MICHAEL ROUILLARD *Trace,* 2001
Acrylic on aluminum, Triptych, 50 x 30 inches overall

DAVID SIMPSON *Dark Iridescent Blue Green,* 1990
Acrylic on canvas mounted on wood, 12 x 12 inches

DAVID SIMPSON *Silver Green,* 1990
Acrylic on canvas mounted on wood, 12 x 12 inches

DAVID SIMPSON *New Primary (Blue),* 1991
Acrylic on canvas mounted on wood, 12 x 12 inches

DAVID SIMPSON *New Primary (Yellow)*, 1991
Acrylic on canvas mounted on wood, 12 x 12 inches

DAVID SIMPSON *Gold Over Green,* 1992
Acrylic on canvas mounted on wood, 12 x 12 inches

DAVID SIMPSON *Study: Yellow Violet Shift,* 1992–1994
Acrylic on canvas mounted on wood, 12 x 12 inches

DAVID SIMPSON *Interference Copper,* 1993
Acrylic on canvas mounted on wood, 12 x 12 inches

DAVID SIMPSON *Sky High*, 1994
Acrylic on canvas, 86 x 72 inches

DAVID SIMPSON *Study: Blue Inversion,* 1994
Acrylic on canvas mounted on wood, 12 x 12 inches

DAVID SIMPSON *Flash Point,* 1996–2003
Acrylic on canvas mounted on wood, 12 x 12 inches

PHIL SIMS *Pieve Caina #7 [cat. 166]*, 1993
Oil on linen mounted on wood, 18 x 16 inches

PHIL SIMS *Not titled [cat. 379]*, 1999
Oil on linen, 38 x 28 inches

LEON POLK SMITH *First-One,* 1954
Oil on cotton duck, 39½-inch diameter

LEON POLK SMITH *Outer Rim,* 1962
Oil on canvas, 68 x 31 inches

HEINER THIEL *MIV/94, #7/9,* 1994
Graphite on steel, 15 ¾ x 15 ¾ inches

HEINER THIEL *MV/94, e.a., Nr. 2,* 1994
Graphite on steel, 15¾ x 15¾ inches

HEINER THIEL *Untitled (Sphere, r=6.6ft.)*, 1998
Anodized aluminum, 38½ x 38½ x 4½ inches

ROY THURSTON *93-4,* 1993
Lacquer on wood, 60 5/16 x 30 5/16 inches

ROY THURSTON *94-1*, 1994
Lacquer on composite panel, Diptych, 30⅜ x 32½ inches each;
30⅜ x 78 inches overall

ROY THURSTON *2001-8,* 2001
Acrylic polyurethane on aluminum, 24 x 19 ¼ inches

ROY THURSTON *2001-16,* 2001
Acrylic polyurethane on aluminum, 23 ¾ x 12 5/16 inches

ROBERT TIEMANN *Not titled,* 1979
Acrylic and cotton twine on canvas, 61¼ x 61½ inches

ROBERT TIEMANN *Not titled,* 1980
Acrylic and cotton twine on canvas, 60 x 60¼ inches

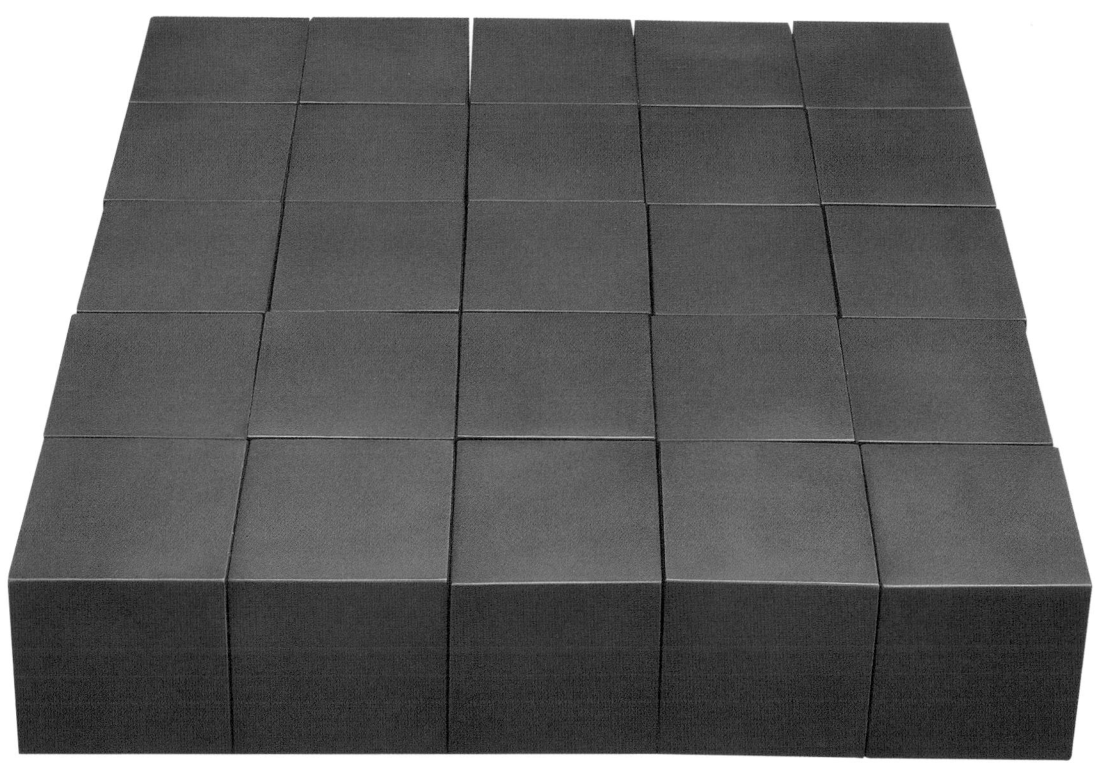

ERIC TILLINGHAST *Not titled,* 1996
Steel, 7 x 30 x 30 inches

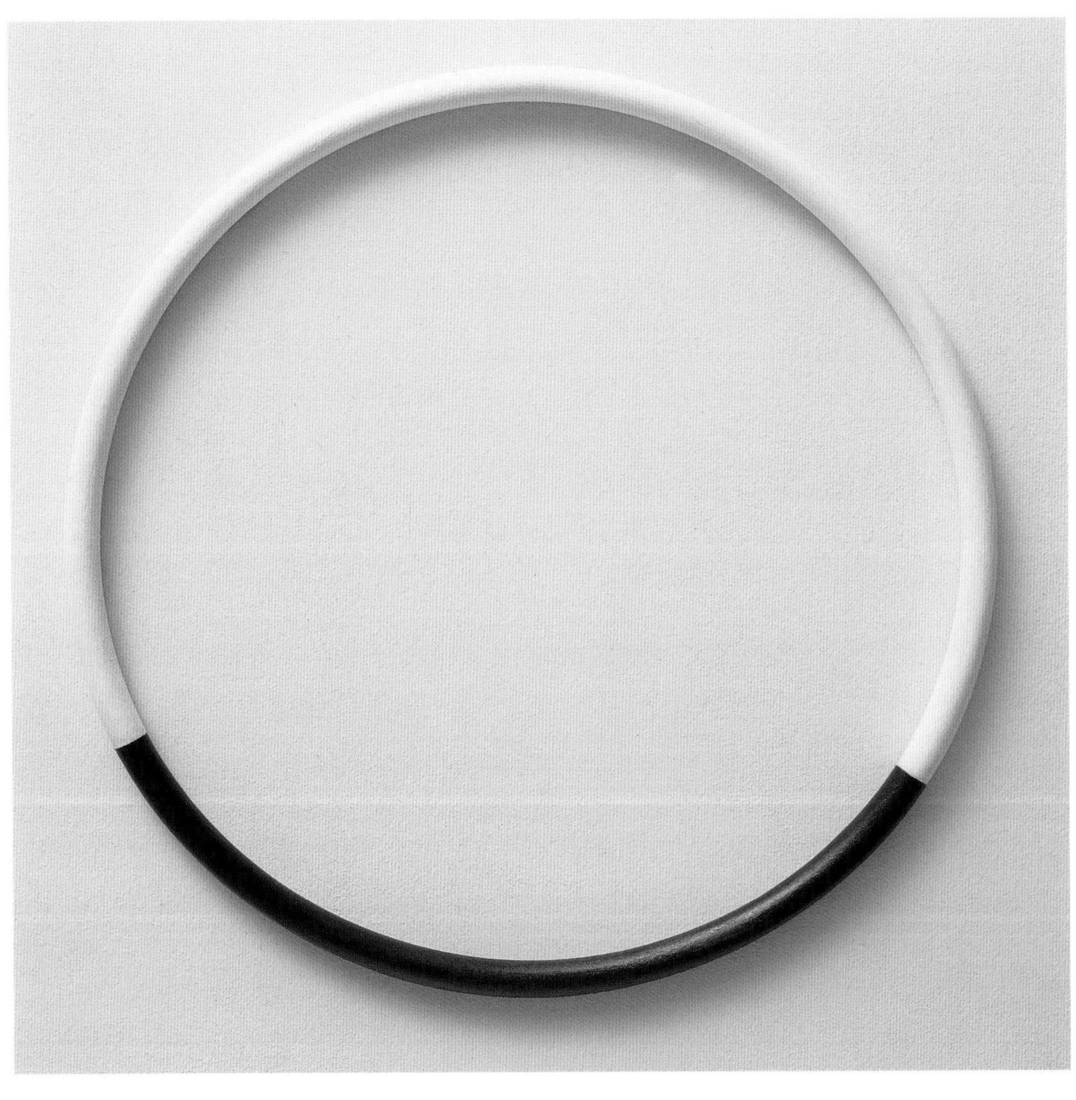

ERIC TILLINGHAST *Ring #1,* 2000
Paint on plastic, 15½-inch diameter x ½ inch

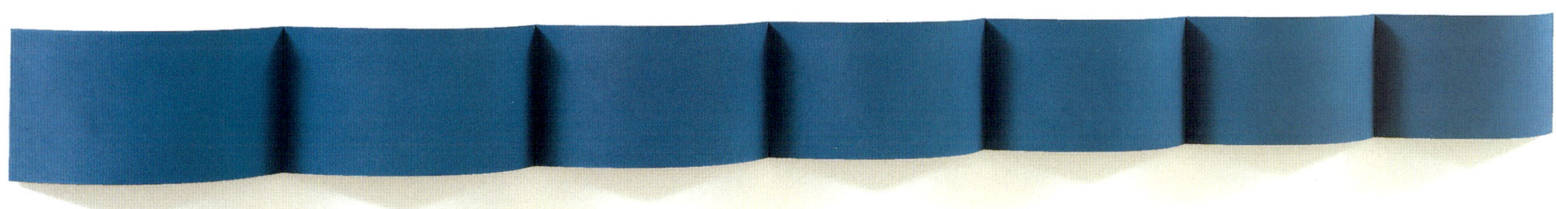

ERIC TILLINGHAST *Aqua Fresh,* 2003
Enamel on steel, 5 x 70 x 5 inches

PETER TOLLENS *Not titled,* 1992–1993
Egg tempera and oil on wood, 12½ x 11¾ inches

PETER TOLLENS *218*, 1996–1997
Egg tempera and oil on wood, 33½ x 31 inches

PETER TOLLENS *230,* 1997
Egg tempera and oil on linen mounted on board, 54½ x 34½ inches

PETER TOLLENS *236,* 1997
Egg tempera and oil on linen mounted on board, 54½ x 42 inches

PETER TOLLENS *271,* 1997–1998
Egg tempera and oil on wood, 27 x 25½ inches

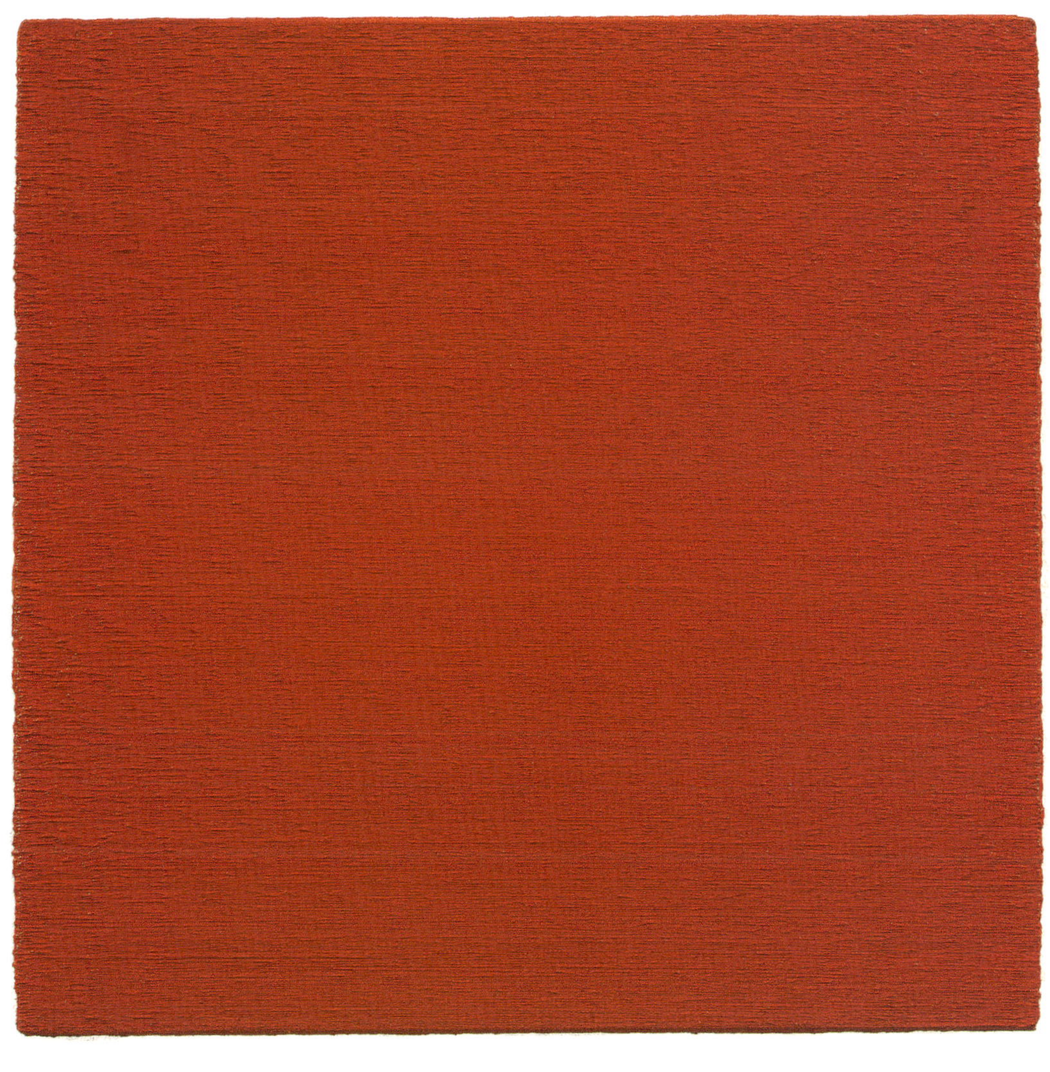

DIETER VILLINGER *Cadmium Orange,* 1997
Oil on canvas mounted on board, 16½ x 16½ inches

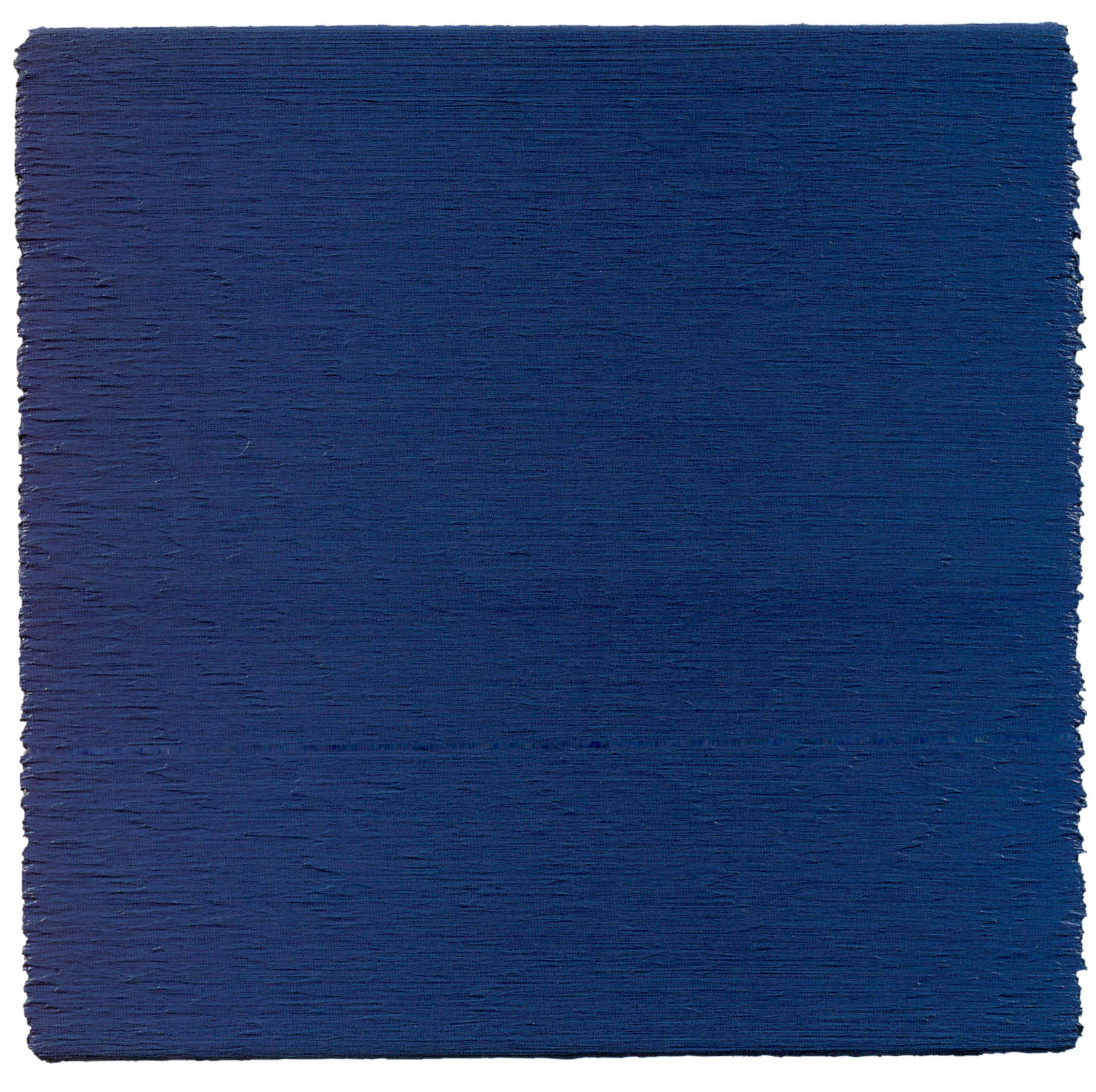

DIETER VILLINGER *Kobaltblau Hell Kobaltblau Turkis,* 1998
Oil on canvas mounted on board, 16½ x 16½ inches

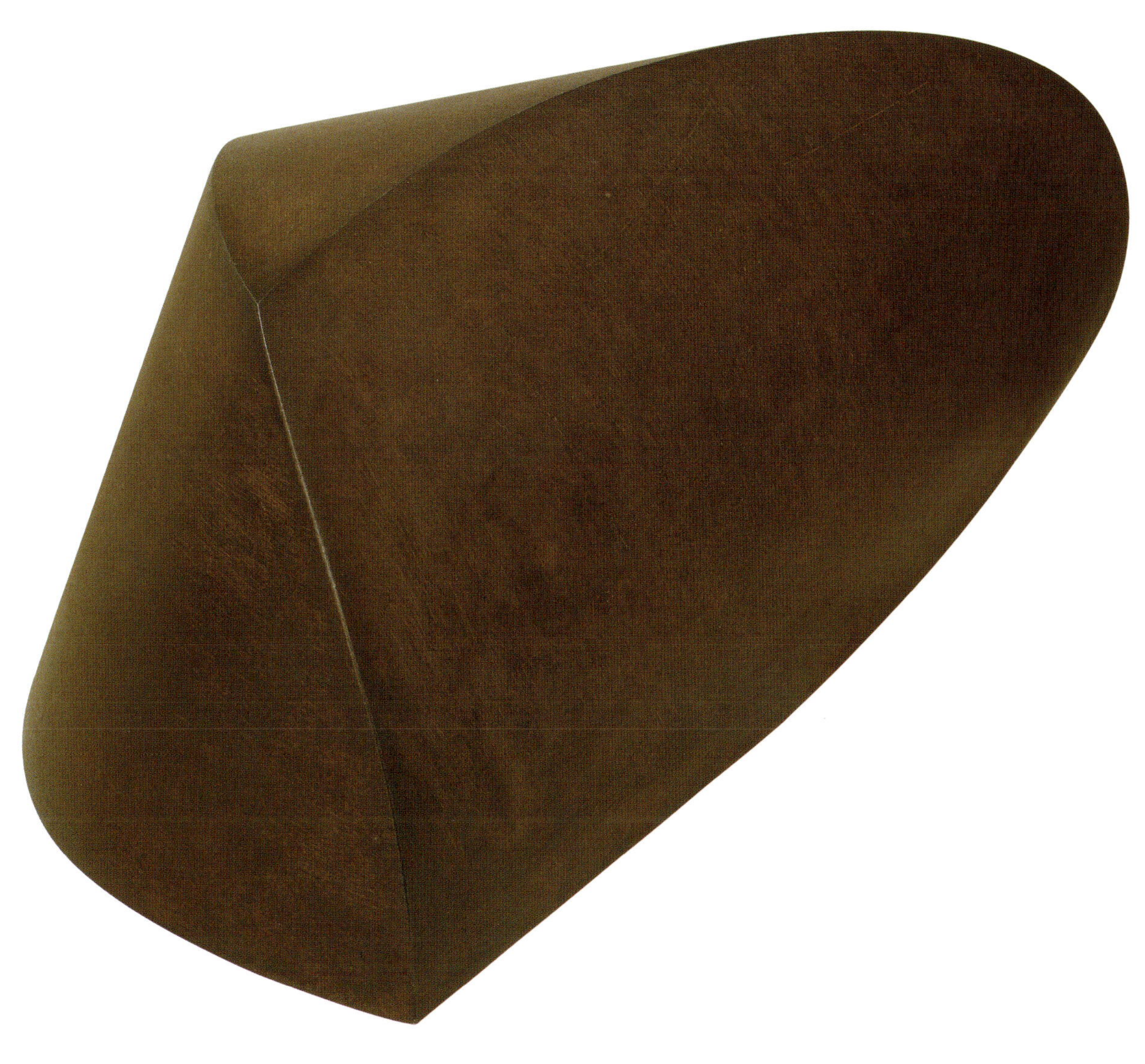

TOM WALDRON *Untitled,* 1997
Steel, 8 x 18 x 9 inches

ALAN WAYNE *#18,* 1994
Oil and alkyd on canvas mounted on board, 27 x 20½ inches

ALAN WAYNE *#19,* 1994
Oil and alkyd on canvas mounted on board, 45 x 34 inches

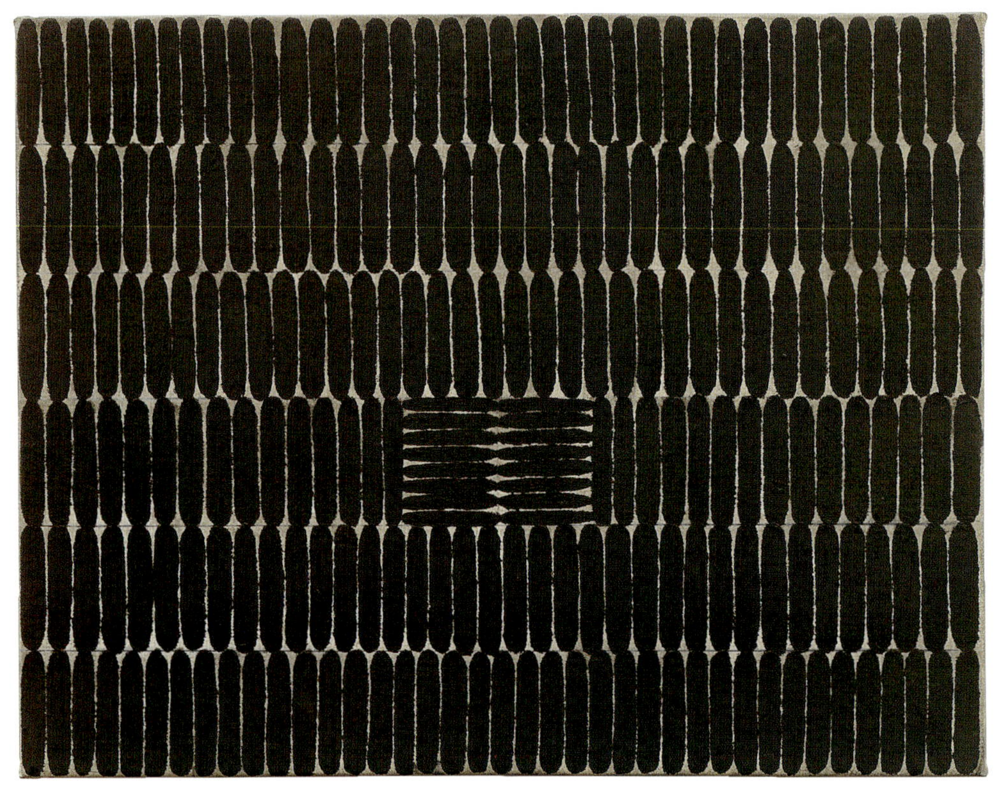

JOAN WITEK *Not titled,* 1980
Oil and graphite on canvas mounted on wood, 24 x 30 inches

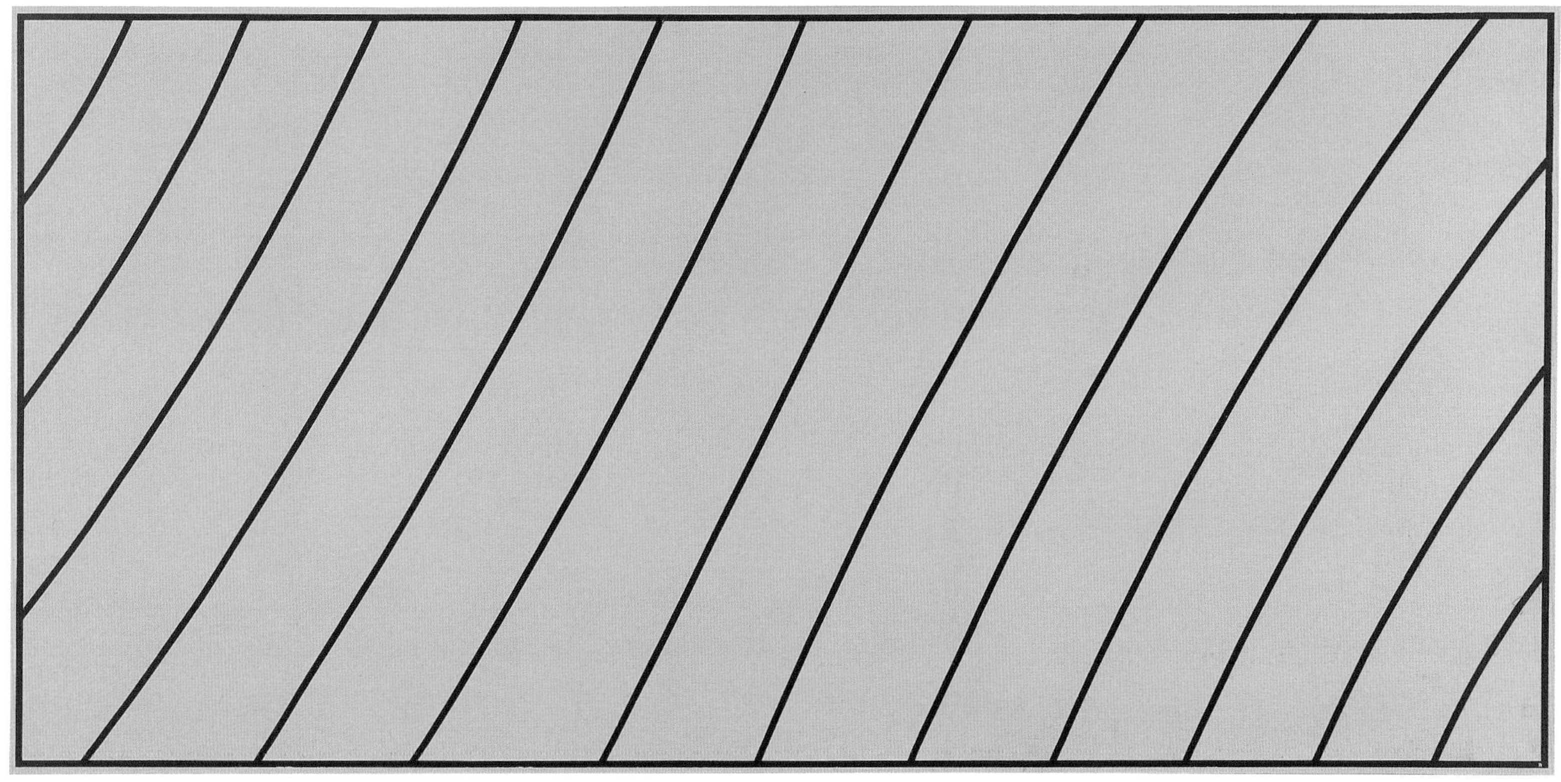

PETER YOUNG *#2,* 1968
Acrylic on canvas, 54 x 108 inches

ON THE ARTISTS

Prepared by Pamela Jones, Susana Tejada, and Margaret Yacobucci

The following selected bibliographies reflect the documentation in the Forman Archives as well as the holdings in The G. Robert Strauss, Jr. Memorial Library, Albright-Knox Art Gallery.

PETER AGOSTINI

Born in New York, New York, 1913
Died in New York, New York, 1993

Contemporary American Sculpture. [New York]: Zabriskie Gallery, 1974. An exhibition catalogue.

Elders of the Tribe. Text by Bernice Steinbaum. New York: Bernice Steinbaum Gallery, 1986. An exhibition catalogue.

Recent American Sculpture. Texts by Hans van Weeren-Griek, Max Kozloff, Dore Ashton, Robert Creeley, Jill Johnston, Henry Geldzahler, Jan van der Marck, and Irving Sandler. New York: The Jewish Museum, 1964. An exhibition catalogue.

65th Annual American Exhibition: Some Directions in Contemporary Painting and Sculpture. Text by A. James Speyer. Chicago: Art Institute of Chicago, 1962. An exhibition catalogue.

Ten American Sculptors. Text by Martin Friedman. Minneapolis: Walker Art Center, 1963. An exhibition catalogue.

White on White. Text by Frederick P. Walkley. Lincoln, MA: De Cordova Museum, 1965. An exhibition catalogue.

JOSEF ALBERS

Born in Bottrop, Germany, 1888
Died in New Haven, Connecticut, 1976

Abstract Trompe L'Oeil. New York: Sidney Janis Gallery, 1965.

Bucher, François and Josef Albers. *Josef Albers: Despite Straight Lines.* rev. ed. Cambridge, MA: MIT Press, 1977.

The Classic Spirit in 20th Century Art: Painters & Sculptors from Brancusi & Mondrian to Today. New York: Sidney Janis Gallery, 1964. An exhibition catalogue.

Josef Albers. Texts by Karl Ruhrberg, Werner Spies, Max Imdahl, Eugen Gomringer, Jürgen Wißmann, Max Bill, R. Buckminster Fuller, and Robert Le Ricolais. Düsseldorf, Germany: Städtische Kunsthalle Düsseldorf, 1970. An exhibition catalogue.

Josef Albers: A National Touring Exhibition for The South Bank Centre 1994. Texts by Henry Meyric Hughes, Ann Jones, Paul Overy, Michael Craig-Martin, and Josef Albers. London: South Bank Centre, 1994. An exhibition catalogue.

Josef Albers: A Retrospective. Texts by Juergen F. Strube, Diane Waldman, Nicholas Fox Weber, Mary Emma Harris, Charles E. Richart, and Neal Benezra. New York: Solomon R. Guggenheim Museum, 1988. An exhibition catalogue.

Josef Albers: Homage to the Square. Texts by René d'Harnoncourt, Kynaston L. McShine, and Josef Albers. New York: The International Council of the Museum of Modern Art, 1964. An exhibition catalogue.

Josef Albers: White Line Squares. Texts by Kenneth E. Tyler, Josef Albers, Henry T. Hopkins, and Gerald Nordland. Los Angeles: Gemini G.E.L., 1966. An exhibition catalogue.

New Paintings by Josef Albers. New York: Sidney Janis, 1968. An exhibition catalogue.

Two Decades of American Painting: An Exhibition Selected by Waldo Rasmussen, The Museum of Modern Art, New York. Texts by Waldo Rasmussen, Irving Sandler, Lucy R. Lippard, and G. R. Swenson. Toyko: National Museum of Modern Art, 1966. An exhibition catalogue.

Umberg, Günter. *Raum für Malerei.* Ostfildern: Cantz Verlag, 1994.

White on White. Text by Frederick P. Walkley. Lincoln, MA: De Cordova Museum, 1965. An exhibition catalogue.

TIMOTHY APP

Born in Akron, Ohio, 1947
Lives in Baltimore, Maryland

Mallinson, Constance. "Timothy App's Abstract Classicism." *Artweek* 10, no. 34 (October 20, 1979): 13.

Timothy App: A Survey of Paintings, 1968–1988. Text by William Peterson. Santa Fe, NM: Linda Durham Gallery, 1988. An exhibition catalogue.

STUART ARENDS

Born in Waterloo, Iowa, 1950
Lives in Roswell, New Mexico

Painting Outside Painting: Biennial Exhibition of Contemporary American Painting. Texts by Jack Cowart and Terrie Sultan; catalogue entries by Maia Damianovic, Eleanor Heartney, Julie Joyce, Jeff Kelley, Leslie King-Hammond, Judith Russi Kirshner, Terry R. Myers, Klaus Ottmann, David Pagel, Barry Schwabsky, and Kathleen Shields. Washington, D.C.: Corcoran Gallery of Art, 1995. An exhibition catalogue.

Stuart Arends: Selected Works 1980–2000. Texts by Wesley Rusnell and John Yau. Roswell, NM: Roswell Museum and Art Center, 2002. An exhibition catalogue.

Stuart Arends: Work 1985–1996. Text by Susan Harris. Santa Fe, NM: The Smith Book Fund, 1998.

Sublime Presence: Stuart Arends, Madeline O'Connor, Florence Pierce, Winston Roeth. Text by Kathleen Shields. Santa Fe, NM: Center for Contemporary Arts of Santa Fe, 1993. An exhibition catalogue.

JOE BARNES

Born in Detroit, Michigan, 1925
Lives in New York, New York

Joe Barnes, James Howell. Text by Marianne Hoffmann. Cologne, Germany: Die Weisse Galerie, 1998. An exhibition catalogue.

Joe Barnes: White Paintings. Text by Jourdan Arpelle. Cologne, Germany: Die Weisse Galerie, 1996. An exhibition catalogue.

Joe Barnes: White Silence; Paintings and Drawings. Text by Florian Goldberg. Cologne, Germany: Die Weisse Galerie, 1994. An exhibition catalogue.

JOHN BEECH

Born in Winchester, England, 1964
Lives in Brooklyn, New York

Blunt Object. Texts by Kimerly Rorschach and Courtenay Smith. Chicago: The David and Alfred Smart Museum of Art, The University of Chicago, 1998. An exhibition catalogue.

From Idea to Matter: Nine Sculptors. Texts by Ted Potter, Edward Albee, and Harry Rand. Richmond, VA: Virginia Commonwealth University, Anderson Gallery, 2000. An exhibition catalogue.

John Beech. Excerpts from conversations with John Beech and Alexander Nagel. San Francisco: Gallery Paule Anglim; New York: Stark Gallery, 2001. An exhibition catalogue.

Painting Outside Painting: Biennial Exhibition of Contemporary American Painting. Texts by Jack Cowart and Terrie Sultan; catalogue entries by Maia Damianovic, Eleanor Heartney, Julie Joyce, Jeff Kelley, Leslie King-Hammond, Judith Russi Kirshner, Terry R. Myers, Klaus Ottmann, David Pagel, Barry Schwabsky, and Kathleen Shields. Washington, D.C.: Corcoran Gallery of Art, 1995. An exhibition catalogue.

TOM BENSON

Born in London, England, 1963
Lives in London, England

A Painting: Stephan Baumkötter, Tom Benson, Andreas Karl Schulze, Ulrich Wellmann. Texts by Jens Peter Koerver and Andrea Edel. Cologne, Germany: Salon Verlag, 2004. An exhibition catalogue.

Tre Rum. Text by David Nessle. Göteborg, Sweden: Göteborgs Konstmuseum, 1986. An exhibition catalogue.

ERIKA BLUMENFELD

Born in Newark, New Jersey, 1971
Lives in Santa Fe, New Mexico

Laird, Scott. "Light Index: Erika Blumenfeld, Ellen Carey, Amanda Means." *Afterimage* 30, no. 5 (2003): [20].

Taylor, Sue. "Review of Exhibitions: Erika Blumenfeld at the Portland Institute for Contemporary Art." *Art in America* 89, no. 9 (2001): 173.

PAUL BOWEN

Born in Colwyn Bay, Wales, United Kingdom, 1951
Lives in Provincetown, Massachusetts

Busa, Christopher. "Paul Bowen." *Arts Magazine* 59, no. 7 (1985): 12.

Paul Bowen. Text by Robyn S. Watson, Tony Vevers, B. H. Friedman, and Sara London. Provincetown, MA: Provincetown Art Association and Museum, 1996. An exhibition catalogue.

MALA BREUER

Born in Oakland, California, 1927
Lives in Santa Fe, New Mexico

Bensley, Lis. "Mala Breuer's Gentle Works Resonate Softly." *Santa Fe New Mexican*, February 2, 1996, sec. *Pasatiempo.*

RODNEY CARSWELL

Born in Carmel, California, 1946
Lives in Gary, Indiana

National Drawing Invitational. Text by Townsend Wolfe. Little Rock: Arkansas Arts Center, 1996. An exhibition catalogue.

New Work: Rodney Carswell. Texts by Thomas R. Toperzer and Buzz Spector with quotations from Rodney Carswell. Norman, OK: University of Oklahoma Museum of Art, Fred Jones Jr. Memorial Art Center, 1988. An exhibition catalogue.

Painting Outside Painting: Biennial Exhibition of Contemporary American Painting. Texts by Jack Cowart and Terrie Sultan; catalogue entries by Maia Damianovic, Eleanor Heartney, Julie Joyce, Jeff Kelley, Leslie King-Hammond, Judith Russi Kirshner, Terry R. Myers, Klaus Ottmann, David Pagel, Barry Schwabsky, and Kathleen Shields. Washington, D.C.: Corcoran Gallery of Art, 1995. An exhibition catalogue.

JOHN CHAMBERLAIN

Born in Rochester, Indiana, 1927
Lives in Shelter Island Heights, New York

Chamberlain. Texts by Johannes Gachnang, R.H. Fuchs, Donald Judd, Robert Creeley, and Kevin Power. Bern, Switzerland: Kunsthalle Bern, 1979. An exhibition catalogue.

The Classic Spirit in 20th Century Art: Painters & Sculptors from Brancusi & Mondrian to Today. New York: Sidney Janis Gallery, 1964. An exhibition catalogue.

John Chamberlain: A Retrospective Exhibition. Text by Diane Waldman. New York: Solomon R. Guggenheim Foundation, 1971. An exhibition catalogue.

John Chamberlain: Early Works. Text by Allan Stone. New York: Allan Stone Gallery, 2003. An exhibition catalogue.

John Chamberlain: Recent Sculpture. Text by Klaus Kertess. New York: PaceWildenstein, 2003. An exhibition catalogue.

Recent American Sculpture. Texts by Hans van Weeren-Griek, Max Kozloff, Dore Ashton, Robert Creeley, Jill Johnston, Henry Geldzahler, Jan van der Marck, and Irving Sandler. New York: The Jewish Museum, 1964. An exhibition catalogue.

65th Annual American Exhibition: Some Directions in Contemporary Painting and Sculpture. Text by A. James Speyer. Chicago: Art Institute of Chicago, 1962. An exhibition catalogue.

Sylvester, Julie. *John Chamberlain: A Catalogue Raisonné of the Sculpture 1954–1985.* New York: Hudson Hills Press in association with the Museum of Contemporary Art, Los Angeles, 1986.

MARK COLE

Born in Houston, Texas, 1955
Lives in New York, New York

Blunt Object. Texts by Kimerly Rorschach and Courtenay Smith. Chicago: The David and Alfred Smart Museum of Art, The University of Chicago, 1998. An exhibition catalogue.

Mark Cole: Paintings. Text by Michael Odom. Marfa, TX and New York: Eugene Binder, 2002. An exhibition catalogue.

JOHN CONNELL

Born in Atlanta, Georgia, 1940
Lives in Ellsworth, Minnesota

The Center for Contemporary Arts Presents The Raft Project: A Collaboration by John Connell and Eugene Newmann. Text by Diane Armitage. Santa Fe, NM: The Center for Contemporary Arts, [1990]. An exhibition catalogue.

The Human Factor: Figurative Sculpture Reconsidered. Texts by Ellen J. Landis, Christopher French, and Kathleen Shields. Albuquerque: Albuquerque Museum, 1993. An exhibition catalogue.

1988 Invitational Exhibition. Text by William D. Ebie. Roswell, NM: Roswell Museum and Art Center, 1988. An exhibition catalogue.

RUDOLF DE CRIGNIS

Born in Winterthur, Switzerland, 1948
Lives in New York, New York

Rudolf de Crignis. Text by Beat Wismer. Zurich, Switzerland: Kunsthalle Winterthur, 1995. An exhibition catalogue.

Rudolf de Crignis: Bilder [Paintings] 1898–1990. Texts by Margit Weinberg Staber and Roman Hollenstein. Translated by Catherine Schelbert. Zurich, Switzerland: Foundation for Constructivist and Concrete Art, 1991. An exhibition catalogue.

Rudolf de Crignis: One Painting. Text by Sabine Muller. Aalst, Belgium: Galerie S65, 1998. An exhibition catalogue.

Rudolf de Crignis: Paintings; An Installation. Text by Gregory Volk. New York: Stark Gallery, 1997. An exhibition brochure.

Visible: Künstlerbücher und Portfolios/Artists' Books and Portfolios. Text by Susanne Bieri. [Geneva, Switzerland]: Prints and Drawings Department of the Swiss National Library, 1998. An exhibition catalogue.

CONSTANCE DEJONG

Born in San Diego, California, 1950
Lives in Albuquerque, New Mexico

The Binational: American Art of the Late 80s. Texts by David Ross, Alan Shestack, Thomas Crow, and Lynne Tillman. Cologne, Germany: Dumont Buchverlag, 1988. An exhibition catalogue.

Reed, Arden. *Constance DeJong: Metal.* Albuquerque: University of New Mexico Press, 2003.

Singular Visions: Contemporary Sculpture in New Mexico. Texts by David Turner, Sandy Ballatore, and the artists. [Santa Fe, NM]: Museum of Fine Arts, Museum of New Mexico, 1991. An exhibition catalogue.

BURGOYNE DILLER

Born in New York, New York, 1906
Died in New York, New York, 1965

Burgoyne Diller. Texts by Jennifer Russell and Barbara Haskell. New York: Whitney Museum of American Art, 1990. An exhibition catalogue.

Burgoyne Diller: Collages. Text by Susan C. Larsen. New York: Michael Rosenfeld Gallery, 1999. An exhibition catalogue.

Burgoyne Diller: Paintings, Sculptures, Drawings. Text by Philip Larson. Minneapolis: Walker Art Center, 1971. An exhibition catalogue.

Burgoyne Diller: The 1930s; Cubism to Abstraction. Text by Francis V. O'Connor. New York: Michael Rosenfeld Gallery, 2002. An exhibition catalogue.

Burgoyne Diller: The Third Dimension; Sculpture and Drawings, 1930–1965. Text by Michael Rosenfeld. New York: Michael Rosenfeld Gallery, 1997. An exhibition catalogue.

The Classic Spirit in 20th Century Art: Painters & Sculptors from Brancusi & Mondrian to Today. New York: Sidney Janis Gallery, 1964. An exhibition catalogue.

Some Assembly Required: Collage Culture in Post-War America. Texts by Sandra Trop, Thomas Piché, Jr., Mark Alice Durant, and Melissa Pearl Fielding. Syracuse, NY: Everson Museum of Art, 2002. An exhibition catalogue.

MARK DI SUVERO

Born in Shanghai, China, 1933
Lives in Long Island City, New York

Humblet, Claudine. *La Nouvelle Abstraction Américaine 1950–1970.* 3 vols. Milan: Skira, 2003.

Mark di Suvero. Text by James K. Monte and Tom Armstrong. New York: Whitney Museum of American Art, 1975. An exhibition catalogue.

Mark di Suvero. Texts by Tilman Osterwold, Sidney Geist, Donald Goddard, and Thomas B. Hess. Stuttgart, Germany: Württembergischer Kunstverein Stuttgart, 1988. An exhibition catalogue.

Mark di Suvero: Orange County. Texts by Naomi Vine and Bruce Guenther. Newport Beach, CA: Orange County Museum of Art, 1998. An exhibition catalogue.

Mark di Suvero: Rétrospective 1959–1991. Texts by Claude Fournet, Marianne Moore, Lao Tseu and Witter Byunner, Gilbert Perlein, Ann Wilson Lloyd, Daniel Dobbels, and Hubert Besacier. Nice, France: Musée d'Art Moderne et d'Art Contemporain, 1991. An exhibition catalogue.

Recent American Sculpture. Texts by Hans van Weeren-Griek, Max Kozloff, Dore Ashton, Robert Creeley, Jill Johnston, Henry Geldzahler, Jan van der Marck, and Irving Sandler. New York: The Jewish Museum, 1964. An exhibition catalogue.

ALAN EBNOTHER

Born in San Francisco, California, 1952
Lives in Stanley, New Mexico

Alan Ebnother: Grun. Text by Robert Walser, George Lawson, and Bernd Growe. Wiesbaden, Germany: Bellevue-Saal, 1992. An exhibition catalogue.

Alan Ebnother: Painting Green. Selected diary entries by Alan Ebnother. Stuttgart, Germany: Galerie Klaus Braun, [2003]. An exhibition catalogue.

ALLAN GRAHAM

Born in San Francisco, California, 1943
Lives in San José, New Mexico

Allan Graham: Fifteen Paintings 1978 and 1979. Text by Laurel Reuter. Santa Fe, NM, 1979. An exhibition catalogue.

Allan Graham/TH: As Real as Thinking. Text by Kathleen Shields. Santa Fe, NM: SITE Santa Fe, 2000. An exhibition catalogue.

Cave of Generation: Allan Graham. Long Island City, NY: Fisher Landau Center; Milan, Italy: Panza de Biumo Collection; Santa Monica, CA: Angles Gallery, 1992. An exhibition catalogue.

The Elusive Surface: Painting in Three Dimensions. Texts by Kathleen Shields and Ellen Landis. Albuquerque: Albuquerque Museum, 1989. An exhibition catalogue.

Graham, Allan. *Allan Graham.* N.p., 1989.

Graham, Allan [Toadhouse, pseud.]. *Shit Floats: Life Goes On.* N.p., 1990.

———. *Visual Eyes: Translations from Toadhouse.* San Francisco: Ethan J. Wagner, 1991.

GLORIA GRAHAM

Born in Beaumont, Texas, 1940
Lives in San José, New Mexico

Bertram, Gabriel. "New Mexico: The Mainstream & Local Currents." *Artnews* 81, no. 4 (1982): 120–24.

Collective Pursuits: Mount Holyoke Investigates Modernism. Texts by Kristen A. Mortimer, Robert L. Herbert, and Paul Staiti. South Hadley, MA: Mount Holyoke College Art Museum, 1993. An exhibition catalogue.

Gloria Graham. Texts by Laurel Meing and Rosalind Constable. Santa Fe, NM: Blue Feather Press, 1980. An exhibition catalogue.

MARCIA HAFIF

Born in Pomona, California, 1929
Lives in New York, New York

Abstract Painting: 1960–69. Texts by Donald Droll, Jane Necol, Carl Andre, Dore Ashton, Gene Baro, Bill Berkson, David Bourdon, Lawrence Campbell, Paul Cummings, E. C. Goossen, Will Insley, Barbara Jakobson, Ellen Johnson, Janet Kardon, Klaus Kertess, Hilton Kramer, Kim Levin, Lucy R. Lippard, Jane Livingston, Linda Nochlin, John Perreault, Robert Rosenblum, Agnes Saalfield, Irving Sandler, Peter Schjeldahl, Holly Solomon, Dorothy Vogel, Carter Ratcliff, David Gigliotti, Fred Riedel, Hollywood DiRusso, Ron Lynch, Billy Kluver, Jerry Kearns, William Hellermann, Carol Squiers, and Donald Kuspit. Long Island City, NY: Institute for Art and Urban Resources, [1983]. An exhibition catalogue.

Afterimage: Drawing Through Process. Texts by Richard Koshalek, Cornelia H. Butler, Pamela M. Lee, and Rebecca Morse. Los Angeles: The Museum of Contemporary Art, Los Angeles, 1999. An exhibition catalogue.

Cooke, Jerry. "Weitere Positionen von Radical Painting in Amerika." *Kunstforum* 88 (1987): 186–89.

Disappearances. Text by Robert C. Morgan. New York: Nahan Contemporary, [1989?]. An exhibition catalogue.

Malerei Pur. Texts by Michael Hübl, Reinhard Ermen, Marcia Hafif, and Rainer Grodnick. Kiel, Germany: Edition Pue, 1991. An exhibition catalogue.

Marcia Hafif. Texts by Sebastian Adler, Germano Celant, and Marcia Hafif. La Jolla, CA: La Jolla Museum of Contemporary Art, 1975. An exhibition catalogue.

Marcia Hafif: Acrylic Glaze Paintings. Text by Marcia Hafif and Ulrich Bischoff. Dresden, Germany: Staatliche Kunstsammlungen; Munich, Germany: Galerie Rupert Walser, 1999. An exhibition catalogue.

Marcia Hafif: Bleistift auf Papier/Pencil on Paper. Text by Andreas Pinczewski. Stuttgart, Germany: Galerie Michael Sturm, 2003. An exhibition catalogue.

Marcia Hafif: Enamel on Wood. Text by Marcia Hafif. Munich, Germany: Galerie Rupert Walser, 1989. An exhibition catalogue.

Marcia Hafif/Erik Saxon. Text by Ulrike Schuck. Otterndorf, Germany: Museum Moderner Kunst Landkreis Cuxhaven, 1994. An exhibition catalogue.

Marcia Hafif: From the Inventory. Text by Elisabeth Grossmann and Marcia Hafif. Zurich, Switzerland: Foundation for Constructivist and Concrete Art, 1995. An exhibition catalogue.

Marcia Hafif: From the Inventory. Text by Sabine Fehlemann, Marcia Hafif, Robert C. Morgan, and Jean-Charles Masséra. Wuppertal, Germany: Kunst-Und Museumsverein, 1994. An exhibition catalogue.

Marcia Hafif: Letters to J-C. Autobiographical letters by Marcia Hafif. Bentheim, Germany: Kunstverein Grafschaft, 1999. An exhibition catalogue.

1973–1998 Artothek. Cologne, Germany: Kölnischen Stadtmuseums, 1998.

Radical Painting. Texts by Thomas Krens, Lilly Wei, Nancy Spector, Joseph Thompson, Tracy Dick, and the artists. Williamstown, MA: Williams College Museum of Art, 1984. An exhibition catalogue.

Umberg, Günter. *Raum für Malerei.* Ostfildern, Germany: Cantz Verlag, 1994.

Wall Painting. Texts by John Hallmark Neff and Judith Russi Kirshner. Chicago: Museum of Contemporary Art, 1979. An exhibition catalogue.

Weinstock, Nino. *Radical Painting und Präsenz der Farbe in den Achtziger Jahren.* Düsseldorf, Germany: Richter Verlag, 2001.

JAMES HAYWARD

Born in San Francisco, California, 1943
Lives in Moorpark, California

Abstract Options. Texts by J. David Farmer, Frances Colpitt, Phyllis Plous, and Rick Orr. Santa Barbara, CA: University Art Museum, 1989. An exhibition catalogue.

Awards in the Visual Arts 10. Texts by Ted Potter and Kathryn Hixon. Winston-Salem, NC: Southeastern Center for Contemporary Art, 1991. An exhibition catalogue.

Plane/Structures. Texts by Anne S. Lasell, Anne Ayres, David Pagel, Dave Hickey, and Joe Scanlan. Los Angeles: Otis Gallery, Otis College of Art and Design, 1994. An exhibition catalogue.

Gilbert-Rolfe, Jeremy. "Abstract Painting and the Historical Object: Considerations on New Paintings by James Hayward." *Arts Magazine* 61, no. 8 (1987): 30–36.

Sunshine and Shadow: Recent Painting in Southern California. Texts by Selma Holo, Gordon F. Hampton, and Susan C. Larson. Los Angeles: Fellows of Contemporary Art, 1985. An exhibition catalogue.

JAMES HOWELL

Born in Kansas City, Missouri, 1935
Lives in New York, New York

James Howell: Gradient Intervals-Series 6.4. Text by Naomi Spector. Santa Fe, NM: Charlotte Jackson Fine Art, 1996. An exhibition catalogue.

James Howell: Series 1.9, Set 68.98. Text by Jan Butterfield. Venice, CA: Sharon Truax Fine Art, 1995. An exhibition catalogue.

James Howell: Series 10. Text by Lilly Wei. Sante Fe, NM: Charlotte Jackson Fine Art, 2000. An exhibition catalogue.

Joe Barnes, James Howell. Text by Marianne Hoffmann. Cologne, Germany: Die Weisse Galerie, 1998. An exhibition catalogue.

JAMES HYDE

Born in Philadelphia, Pennsylvania, 1958
Lives in Brooklyn, New York

James Hyde. Text by David Carrier. New York: John Good Gallery, 1989. An exhibition catalogue.

James Hyde 1991/94. Texts by Joseph Masheck, David Kaufmann, Thomas Zummer, Elke Uebel, and Jimmy Raskin. New York: John Good Gallery; Nürnberg, Germany: Galerie Art In, 1994. An exhibition catalogue.

Painting Outside Painting: Biennial Exhibition of Contemporary American Painting. Texts by Jack Cowart and Terrie Sultan; catalogue entries by Maia Damianovic, Eleanor Heartney, Julie Joyce, Jeff Kelley, Leslie King-Hammond, Judith Russi Kirshner, Terry R. Myers, Klaus Ottmann, David Pagel, Barry Schwabsky, and Kathleen Shields. Washington, D.C.: Corcoran Gallery of Art, 1995. An exhibition catalogue.

RACHEL LACHOWICZ

Born in San Francisco, California, 1964
Lives in Santa Monica, California

Porges, Maria. "Rachel Lachowicz." *Artforum* 31, no. 5 (1993): 80.

Sense and Sensibility: Women Artists and Minimalism in the Nineties. Text by Lynn Zelevansky. New York: Museum of Modern Art, 1994. An exhibition catalogue.

JODY LOMBERG

Born in Englewood, New Jersey, 1956
Lives in New York, New York

Painting Outside Painting: Biennial Exhibition of Contemporary American Painting. Texts by Jack Cowart and Terrie Sultan; catalogue entries by Maia Damianovic, Eleanor Heartney, Julie Joyce, Jeff Kelley, Leslie King-Hammond, Judith Russi Kirshner, Terry R. Myers, Klaus Ottmann, David Pagel, Barry Schwabsky, and Kathleen Shields. Washington, D.C.: Corcoran Gallery of Art, 1995. An exhibition catalogue.

ED MALINA

Born in Long Island City, New York, 1952
Lives in Burdette, New York

Grove, Nancy. "Arts Reviews: Ed Malina." *Arts Magazine* 50, no. 7 (1976): 14–15.

JOSEPH MARIONI

Born in Cincinnati, Ohio, 1943
Lives in New York, New York

Abstrakte Malerei Zwischen Analyse und Synthese. Texts by Rosemarie Schwarzwälder, Philipp Schönborn, Noemi Smolik, Joseph Marioni, Adrian Schiess, Heinrich Dunst, Perry Roberts, Lydia Dona, Helmut Federle, David Reed, John Zinsser, and Stephen Ellis. Vienna, Austria: Galerie Nächst St. Stephan, Rosemarie Schwarzwälder, 1992. An exhibition catalogue.

Color: Four Painters: Max Gimblett, Joseph Marioni, Phil Sims, Thornton Willis. Texts by Jesse Murry and Victoria Oscarsson. New York: Oscarsson Hood Gallery, 1981. An exhibition catalogue.

Joseph Marioni: Blue Paintings. Texts by Howard Yezerski, Joseph Marioni, and Carl Belz. Boston: Howard Yezerski Gallery, 2002. An exhibition catalogue.

Joseph Marioni, Erik Saxon, Günter Umberg, Ulrich Wellmann. Texts by Johannes Teiser, Georg Imdahl, Erik Saxon, Richard Hoppe-Sailer, and Roland Scotti. Arnsberg, Germany: Kunstverein Arnsberg, 1991. An exhibition catalogue.

Joseph Marioni: Four Paintings. Texts by Ross Searle, David Pestorius, and Rex Butler. Brisbane, Australia: University Art Museum, University of Queensland, 2000. An exhibition catalogue.

Joseph Marioni: IRO. Text by Stephen Addiss and Patrick McCracken. [New York]: thepainter.net, 2002. An exhibition catalogue.

Joseph Marioni: Painter. Text by Henry Staten. Aalst, Belgium: Galerij S65, 1989. An exhibition catalogue.

Joseph Marioni: Painter. Text by Irwin M. Lippman, Annegreth Nill, and Charles Dee Mitchell. Columbus, OH: Columbus Museum of Art, 1999.

Joseph Marioni: Painter. Text by Joseph Marioni. Aalst, Belgium: Gallery S65, 1994. An exhibition catalogue.

Joseph Marioni: Painter. Texts by Justus Jonas, Joseph Marioni, and Hannelore Kersting. [Mönchengladbach, Germany]: Städtisches Museum Abteiberg Mönchengladbach, 1994. An exhibition catalogue.

Joseph Marioni, Painter: Works on Paper. Text by Georg Imdahl. Aalst, Belgium: Gallery S65, 1997. An exhibition catalogue.

Joseph Marioni: Paintings 1970–1998; A Survey. Text by Carl Belz and Barbara Rose. Waltham, MA: Rose Art Museum, Brandeis University, 1998. An exhibition catalogue.

Joseph Marioni: Paintings 1977–1994. Text by Werner Würtinger and Stefan Gronert. Vienna, Austria: Wiener Secession, 1996. An exhibition catalogue.

Joseph Marioni; Private Icons. Texts by Jochen Poetter and Charles Altieri. Baden-Baden, Germany: Staatliche Kunsthalle Baden-Baden, 1995. An exhibition catalogue.

Joseph Marioni: Triptych. Texts by Stefan Kraus and Joseph Marioni in conversation with Katharina Winnekes. Cologne, Germany: Diözesanmuseum, 1999. An exhibition catalogue.

Kersting, Hannelore. *Joseph Marioni: Painter.* Extended and rev. ed. Mönchengladbach, Germany: Städtisches Museum Abteiberg Mönchengladbach, 1994.

Malerei Pur. Texts by Michael Hübl, Reinhard Ermen, Marcia Hafif, and Rainer Grodnick. Kiel, Germany: Edition Pue, 1991. An exhibition catalogue.

Marioni, Joseph. "Der Ursprüngliche Ort der Malerei." *Kunstforum* 88 (1987): 184–85, 189–90.

Monochromie Geometrie. Texts by Johannes Meinhardt, Erich Franz, Imi Knoebel, Ingvild Goetz, Robert Nickas, and Rolf Hengesbach. Munich, Germany: Sammlung Goetz, 1996. An exhibition catalogue.

Outside the Cartouche: Zur Frage des Betrachters in der Radikalen Malerei. Text by Rupert Walser. Munich, Germany: Neue Kunst Verlag, 1986. An exhibition catalogue.

Peinture Radicale. Text by Amine Haase. Rennes, France: La Criée, 1988. An exhibition catalogue.

Pleasures of Sight and States of Being: Radical Abstract Painting Since 1900. Texts by Allys Palladino-Craig and Roald Nasgaard. Tallahassee, FL: Florida State University Museum of Fine Arts, 2001. An exhibition catalogue.

Präsenz der Farbe Radical Painting: 13 Maler im Verein für Aktuelle Kunst Oberhausen. Texts by Hartwig Kompa and Amine Haase. Oberhausen, Germany: Verein für Aktuelle Kunst, 1984. An exhibition catalogue.

Radical Painting. Text by Thomas Krens, Lilly Wei, Nancy Spector, Joseph Thompson, Tracy Dick, and the artists. Williamstown, MA: Williams College Museum of Art, 1984. An exhibition catalogue.

Staten, Henry. "Joseph Marioni: Malerei Jenseits von Narrativität." *Kunstforum* 88 (1987): 177–83.

Umberg, Günter. *Raum für Malerei.* Ostfildern, Germany: Cantz Verlag, 1994.

Weinstock, Nino. *Radical Painting und Präsenz der Farbe in den Achtziger Jahren.* Düsseldorf, Germany: Richter Verlag, 2001.

ALLAN MCCOLLUM

Born in Los Angeles, California, 1944
Lives in New York, New York

Allan McCollum. Text by Andrea Fraser and Ulrich Wilmes. Cologne, Germany: Walther König, 1988. An exhibition catalogue.

Allan McCollum. Texts by Anne Rorimer. Lynne Cooke, and Selma Klein Essink. Eindhoven, The Netherlands: Stedelijk Van Abbemuseum; London, England: Serpentine Gallery; Valencia, Spain: IVAM Centre del Carme, 1989. An exhibition catalogue.

Allan McCollum: Perfect Vehicles 1988. Texts by Laurence J. Ruggiero and [Joseph Jacobs]. Sarasota, FL: John and Mable Ringling Museum of Art, 1988. An exhibition catalogue.

Allan McCollum: Surrogates. Text by Craig Owens. London, England: Lisson Gallery, 1985. An exhibition catalogue.

Artschwager: His Peers and Persuasion, 1963–1988. Texts by Daniel Weinberg and Klaus Kertess. Los Angeles: Daniel Weinberg Gallery, 1988. An exhibition catalogue.

Culture Medium: Sophie Calle, Sarah Charlesworth, Donigan Cumming, Dieter Froese, Allan McCollum, Angela Neuke. Texts by Charles Stainback, Sophie Calle, Sarah Charlesworth, Donigan Cumming, Dieter Froese, Allan McCollum, and Angela Neuke. New York: International Center of Photography, 1989. An exhibition catalogue.

Damaged Goods: Desire and the Economy of the Object. Texts by Marcia Tucker, Brian Wallis, Gretchen Bender, Allan McCollum, Hal Foster, Louise Lawler, Haim Steinbach, Justen Ladda, Barbara Bloom, Deborah Bershad, Jeff Koons, Andrea Fraser, Judith Barry, Ken Lum, and Claire Dannenbaum. New York: The New Museum of Contemporary Art, 1986. An exhibition catalogue.

Knight, Christopher. *Last Chance for Eden.* Los Angeles: Art Issues Press, 1995.

Richards, Judith Olch. *Inside the Studio: Two Decades of Talks With Artists in New York.* New York: Independent Curators International, 2004.

JOHN MEYER

Born in Louisville, Kentucky, 1943
Died in San Francisco, California, 2002

Fucare: To Paint Red; John Meyer. Text by Lilly Wei. San Francisco, 1987. An exhibition catalogue.

John Meyer: Diptychs. Texts by Erich Franz, John Meyer, and Gabriele Kübler. Reutlingen, Germany: Stiftung für Konkrete Kunst, 1996. An exhibition catalogue.

SECA Art Award 1990: Nayland Blake, John Meyer. Texts by John R. Lane and John Caldwell. San Francisco: San Francisco Museum of Modern Art, 1990. An exhibition catalogue.

PATRICIA MOISAN

Born in Washington, D.C., 1951
Lives in Pasadena, California

Patricia Moisan: Blue and Red Paintings. Text by Patricia Moisan. Düsseldorf, Germany: Druckerei Heinrich Winterscheidt GmbH, 1991.

DOUG OHLSON

Born in Cherokee, Iowa, 1936
Lives in New York, New York

Abstract Painting: 1960–69. Texts by Donald Droll, Jane Necol, Carl Andre, Dore Ashton, Gene Baro, Bill Berkson, David Bourdon, Lawrence Campbell, Paul Cummings, E. C. Goossen, Will Insley, Barbara Jakobson, Ellen Johnson, Janet Kardon, Klaus Kertess, Hilton Kramer, Kim Levin, Lucy R. Lippard, Jane Livingston, Linda Nochlin, John Perreault, Robert Rosenblum, Agnes Saalfield, Irving Sandler, Peter Schjeldahl, Holly Solomon, Dorothy Vogel, Carter Ratcliff, David Gigliotti, Fred Riedel, Hollywood DiRusso, Ron Lynch, Billy Kluver, Jerry Kearns, William Hellermann, Carol Squiers, and Donald Kuspit. Long Island City, NY: Institute for Art and Urban Resources, [1983]. An exhibition catalogue.

Doug Ohlson at Bennington: Two Decades 1962–1982. Text by E. C. Goossen. Bennington, VT: Suzanne Lemberg Usday Gallery, Bennington College, 1982. An exhibition catalogue.

Doug Ohlson: Paintings 1984–1985. Text by Steven Henry Madoff. New York: Ruth Siegel, Ltd., 1985. An exhibition catalogue.

Doug Ohlson: 20 Years of Painting: 1982–2002. Texts by Richard Stapleford, Michael Brennan, E. C. Goossen, and an interview with the artist. New York: Hunter College, Times Square Gallery, 2002. An exhibition catalogue.

FLORENCE PIERCE

Born in Washington, D.C., 1918
Lives in Albuquerque, New Mexico

Ashman, Stuart, and Suzanne Deats. *Abstract Art: The New Mexico Artist Series.* Albuquerque, NM: Fresco Fine Art Publications, 2003.

In Pursuit of Perfection: The Art of Agnes Martin, Maria Martinez, and Florence Pierce. Texts by Marsha C. Bol, Lucy R. Lippard, and Timothy Robert Rodgers. Santa Fe, NM: Museum of Fine Arts, Santa Fe, 2004.

Lippard, Lucy, and Florence Pierce. *Florence Pierce: In Touch With Light.* Santa Fe, NM: Smith Book Fund, 1998.

Postmark: An Abstract Effect. Texts by Louis Grachos, Bruce W. Ferguson, David Moos, and David Pagel. Santa Fe, NM: SITE Santa Fe, 1999. An exhibition catalogue.

Sublime Presence: Stuart Arends, Madeline O'Connor, Florence Pierce, Winston Roeth. Text by Kathleen Shields. Santa Fe, NM: Center for Contemporary Arts of Santa Fe, 1993. An exhibition catalogue.

WINSTON ROETH

Born in Chicago, Illinois, 1945
Lives in Beacon, New York

Roeth, Winston. "Winston Roeth: The Speed of Light; Monologue." *Hudson River Art* 3 (2004): 4–8.

Sublime Presence: Stuart Arends, Madeline O'Connor, Florence Pierce, Winston Roeth. Text by Kathleen Shields. Santa Fe, NM: Center for Contemporary Arts of Santa Fe, 1993. An exhibition catalogue.

Weinstock, Nino. *Radical Painting und Präsenz der Farbe in den Achtziger Jahren.* Düsseldorf, Germany: Richter Verlag, 2001.

Winston Roeth. Text by Tom McDonough. [Auckland, New Zealand]: Ouroborus Publishing, 2002.

Winston Roeth. Texts by Giuseppe Panza di Biumo and Jan Avgikos. New York: Stark Gallery and Göteborg, Sweden: Ars Nova Galleri, 1993. An exhibition catalogue.

MICHAEL ROUILLARD

Born in Valparaiso, Florida, 1955
Lives in New York, New York

Wei, Lilly. "Michael Rouillard at Stark." *Art in America* 83, no. 6 (1995): 105–06.

DAVID SIMPSON

Born in Pasadena, California, 1928
Lives in Berkeley, California

David Simpson. Interview with the artist by Reinhard Ermen and text by Sabine Müller. Cologne, Germany: Renate Schröder Galerie, 2002. An exhibition catalogue.

2002 Artothek. Cologne, Germany: Kölnischen Stadtmuseums, 2002.

David Simpson. Text by Kenneth Baker. Verona, Italy: Studio La Città, 2001. An exhibition catalogue.

David Simpson. Texts by David Bonetti and Michael Haggerty. Verona, Italy: Studio La Città, 1997. An exhibition catalogue.

David Simpson 1957–1967. Text by John Humphrey. San Francisco: San Francisco Museum of Art, [1967]. An exhibition catalogue.

David Simpson: Paintings. Texts by Harvey L. Jones, George W. Neubert, and David Simpson. Oakland, CA: Oakland Museum, 1978. An exhibition catalogue.

PHIL SIMS

Born in Richmond, California, 1940
Lives in Lakewood, Pennsylvania

Color: Four Painters: Max Gimblett, Joseph Marioni, Phil Sims, Thornton Willis. Texts by Jesse Murry and Victoria Oscarsson. New York: Oscarsson Hood Gallery, 1981. An exhibition catalogue.

Malerei Pur. Texts by Michael Hübl, Reinhard Ermen, Marcia Hafif, and Rainer Grodnick. Kiel, Germany: Edition Pue, 1991. An exhibition catalogue.

1973–1998 Artothek. Cologne, Germany: Kölnischen Stadtmuseums, 1998.

Phil Sims at Galerie Rupert Walser. Text by Erich Franz. Munich, Germany: Galerie Rupert Walser, 1997. An exhibition catalogue.

Phil Sims: Marienbad Paintings. Texts by Ralf Beil and Martin Engler and interview with the artist by Ralf Beil and Martin Engler. Freiburg, Germany: Ausstellungshalle Marienbad, 1996. An exhibition catalogue

Phil Sims: Paintings. Text by John Yau. Santa Fe, NM: Charlotte Jackson Fine Art, 2000. An exhibition catalogue.

Phil Sims: Paintings. Text by Stephan Berg. Badenweiler, Germany: Galerie Krohn, 2001. An exhibition catalogue.

Phil Sims: Umbrian Paintings. Notes on Pieve Caina by Michele Meyers. Munich, Germany: Galerie Rupert Walser, 1993. An exhibition catalogue.

Radical Painting. Text by Thomas Krens, Lilly Wei, Nancy Spector, Joseph Thompson, Tracy Dick, and the artists. Williamstown, MA: Williams College Museum of Art, 1984. An exhibition catalogue.

Umberg, Günter. *Raum für Malerei*. Ostfildern, Germany: Cantz Verlag, 1994.

Weinstock, Nino. *Radical Painting und Präsenz der Farbe in den Achtziger Jahren*. Düsseldorf, Germany: Richter Verlag, 2001.

LEON POLK SMITH

Born in Chickasha, Oklahoma, 1906
Died in New York, New York, 1996

The Classic Spirit in 20th Century Art: Painters & Sculptors from Brancusi & Mondrian to Today. New York: Sidney Janis Gallery, 1964. An exhibition catalogue.

Humblet, Claudine. *La Nouvelle Abstraction Américaine 1950–1970*. 3 vols. Milan: Skira, 2003.

Leon Polk Smith. Text by Lawrence Alloway. San Francisco: San Francisco Museum of Art, 1968. An exhibition catalogue.

Leon Polk Smith. Texts by Nicolas Calas and Elena Calas. New York: Galerie Denise René, 1973. An exhibition catalogue.

Leon Polk Smith. Texts by Serge Lemoine, Bernhard Holeczek, and Jean-Paul Monery. Ludwigshafen am Rhein, Germany: Wilhelm-Hack-Museum, 1989. An exhibition catalogue.

Leon Polk Smith: American Painter. Texts by Robert T. Buck, Carter Ratcliff, Brooke Kamin Rapaport, Arthur C. Danto, and John Alan Farmer. Brooklyn, NY: Brooklyn Museum, 1996. An exhibition catalogue.

Leon Polk Smith: Collagen 1981–1983. Texts by Dieter Honisch and Lucius Grisebach. Berlin, Germany: Nationalgalerie Berlin Staatliche Museen Preußischer Kulturbesitz, 1984. An exhibition catalogue.

Leon Polk Smith: Collages 1954–1986. Texts by Serge Lemoine and Christine Poullain. Grenoble, France: Musée de Grenoble, 1998. An exhibition catalogue.

Leon Polk Smith: 5 Decades of Geometric Inventions. Text by Carter Ratcliff. New York: DiLaurenti Gallery, 1987. An exhibition catalogue.

Leon Polk Smith: Paintings of the Nineties. Text by Jason McCoy. New York: Jason McCoy, Inc., 1997. An exhibition catalogue.

Leon Polk Smith: Selected Works 1943–1992; Promised Gift to The Brooklyn Museum. Text by Robert T. Buck. Brooklyn, NY: Brooklyn Museum, 1993.

65th Annual American Exhibition: Some Directions in Contemporary Painting and Sculpture. Text by A. James Speyer. Chicago: Art Institute of Chicago, 1962. An exhibition catalogue.

White on White. Text by Frederick P. Walkley. Lincoln, MA: De Cordova Museum, 1965. An exhibition catalogue.

HEINER THIEL

Born in Bernkastel-Kues, Germany, 1957
Lives in Wiesbaden, Germany

Heiner Thiel: Wandobjekte und Zeichnungen 1997–1998/ Wall-objects and drawings 1997–1998. Text by Matthias Bleyl. Mainz, Germany: Galerie Alf-Krister Job, 1998. An exhibition catalogue.

Heiner Thiel: Wandobjekt Zeichnung, Balmoral-Stipendium 1998. Text by Daniela Christmann. Bad Ems, Germany: Künstlerhaus Schloss Balmoral, 1998.

ROY THURSTON

Born in Huntington, New York, 1949
Lives in Los Angeles, California

Plane/Structures. Texts by Anne S. Lasell, Anne Ayres, David Pagel, Dave Hickey, and Joe Scanlan. Los Angeles: Otis Gallery, Otis College of Art and Design, 1994. An exhibition catalogue.

Quiet: George Lawson, Dennis Leon, Shauna Peck, Yoshitomo Saito, Roy Thurston. Texts by Harvey L. Jones and Paul Tomidy. Oakland, CA: Oakland Museum, 1989. An exhibition catalogue.

Roy Thurston. Text by Peter Clothier. West Hollywood, CA: Chac Mool Gallery, [2002]. An exhibition catalogue.

ROBERT TIEMANN

Born in Austin, Texas, 1936
Lives in San Antonio, Texas

Contemporary Works Series, 1982: Mark Pritchett, Robert Tiemann. San Antonio, TX: San Antonio Museum Association, [1982]. An exhibition catalogue.

Robert Tiemann. Text by Martha Utterback. Austin, TX: University Art Museum, University of Texas, 1967. An exhibition catalogue.

Scaljon, Basil. "Formalist Icons." *Artweek* 10, no. 44 (December 29, 1979): 17.

ERIC TILLINGHAST

Born in Los Angeles, California, 1974
Lives in Santa Fe, New Mexico

Sullivan, Craig. "Minimalist Finds Poetry in Water." *Albuquerque Journal*, June 9, 2000.

PETER TOLLENS

Born in Kleve, Germany, 1954
Lives in Cologne, Germany

Bleyl, Matthias. "Jüngstepositionen Radikaler Malerei in Deutschland." *Kunstforum* 88 (1987): 159–69.

In-Between. Text by Karin Stempel. Lüdenscheid, Germany: Museen der Stadt Lüdenscheid, 1992. An exhibition catalogue.

Peter Tollens. Text by Stefan Kraus. Aalst, Belgium: Galerie S65, 2001. An exhibition catalogue.

Peter Tollens. Texts by Stefan Kraus and Karin Stempel. Cologne, Germany: Galerie G, 1995. An exhibition catalogue.

Peter Tollens: Zwischen zwei Deckeln; Zeichnungen in Heften, Kladden und Büchern. Text by Stefan Kraus. Cologne, Germany: Artillerie, 1994. An exhibition catalogue.

Präsenz der Farbe Radical Painting: 13 Maler im Verein für Aktuelle Kunst Oberhausen. Texts by Hartwig Kompa and Amine Haase. Oberhausen, Germany: Verein für Aktuelle Kunst, 1984. An exhibition catalogue.

Weinstock, Nino. *Radical Painting und Präsenz der Farbe in den Achtziger Jahren.* Düsseldorf, Germany: Richter Verlag, 2001.

Werkbuch Peter Tollens. Cologne, Germany: Diözesanmuseum Köln, 2001.

DIETER VILLINGER

Born in Bad Bergzabern, Germany, 1947
Lives in Munich, Germany

Bleyl, Matthias. "Jüngstepositionen Radikaler Malerei in Deutschland." *Kunstforum* 88 (1987): 159–69.

Dieter Villinger. Text by Michael Hübl. Munich, Germany: Kulturreferat der Landeshauptstadt, 1989. An exhibition catalogue.

Dieter Villinger: Die Anwesenheit der Farbe. Munich and Cologne, Germany: Reinhard Ermen, 1986.

Dieter Villinger: Gelb.Blau; Installation für die Fachhochschule Landshut. Text by Michael Hübl. Nürnberg, Germany: Institut für moderne Kunst Nürnberg, 2002.

Dieter Villinger: Malerei. Texts by Andreas Vowinckel and Bernd Growe. Karlsruhe, Germany: Badischer Kunstverein, 1991. An exhibition catalogue.

Dieter Villinger: Malerei. Texts by Heinz Höfchen and Matthias Bleyl. Kaiserslautern, Germany: Pfalzgalerie Kaiserslautern, 1993. An exhibition catalogue.

Farbe als Farbe. Texts by Reinhard Ermen, Helmut Friedel, and Marcia Hafif. Munich, Germany: Städtische Galerie im Lenbachhaus München, 1989. An exhibition catalogue.

Präsenz der Farbe Radical Painting: 13 Maler im Verein für Aktuelle Kunst Oberhausen. Texts by Hartwig Kompa and Amine Haase. Oberhausen, Germany: Verein für Aktuelle Kunst, 1984. An exhibition catalogue.

Umberg, Günter. *Raum für Malerei.* Ostfildern, Germany: Cantz Verlag, 1994.

Weinstock, Nino. *Radical Painting und Präsenz der Farbe in den Achtziger Jahren.* Düsseldorf, Germany: Richter Verlag, 2001.

TOM WALDRON

Born in Minneapolis, Minnesota, 1953
Lives in Corrales, New Mexico

Kuspit, Donald. "Tom Waldron." *Artforum* 40, no. 8 (2002): 140.

Peterson, William. "Ten for the '90s: Albuquerque; Tom Waldron." *ARTnews* 89, no. 4 (1990): 152.

Singular Visions: Contemporary Sculpture in New Mexico. Texts by David Turner, Sandy Ballatore, and the artists. [Santa Fe, NM]: Museum of Fine Arts, Museum of New Mexico, 1991. An exhibition catalogue.

ALAN WAYNE

Born in Los Angeles, California, 1949
Lives in Los Angeles, California

Plane / Structures. Texts by Anne S. Lasell, Anne Ayres, David Pagel, Dave Hickey, and Joe Scanlan. Los Angeles: Otis Gallery, Otis College of Art and Design, 1994. An exhibition catalogue.

JOAN WITEK

Born in New York, New York, 1943
Lives in New York, New York

Joan Witek. Texts by John R. Lane and John Caldwell. Pittsburgh, PA: Museum of Art, Carnegie Institute, 1984. An exhibition catalogue.

Joan Witek: Drawings. Text by David Carrier. New York: Wynn Kramarsky, 1997. An exhibition catalogue.

Joan Witek: New Paintings. Text by Lilly Wei. New York: N.p., 2000. An exhibition catalogue.

PETER YOUNG

Born in Pittsburgh, Pennsylvania, 1940
Lives in Bisbee, Arizona

Eight Artists: Dan Christensen, Neil Jenney, Don Judd, Roy Lichtenstein, Robert Rauschenberg, Gary Stephan, Cy Twombly, Peter Young. Text by David Whitney. Corpus Christi: Art Museum of South Texas, 1974. An exhibition catalogue.

Six Painters: Edward Avedisian, Darby Bannard, Dan Christensen, Ron Davis, Larry Poons, Peter Young. Texts by Gordon M. Smith and James N. Wood. Buffalo, NY: Albright-Knox Art Gallery, 1971. An exhibition catalogue.

CATALOGUE

OF THE PAINTING AND SCULPTURE COLLECTION

All works shown in boldface are included in the exhibition at the Albright-Knox Art Gallery, May 6 – July 3, 2005.

Height precedes width and depth.

PETER AGOSTINI

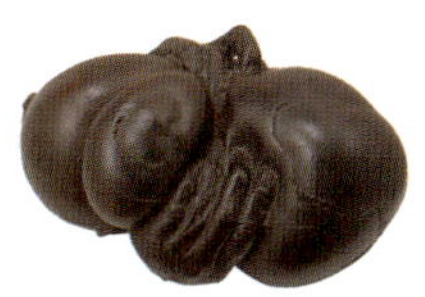

Squeeze, 1963
Bronze
7 x 14 x 10 in. (17.7 x 35.5 x 25.4 cm.)
Purchased from Richard Gray Gallery, Chicago, Illinois, 1966
Promised Gift of Natalie and Irving Forman

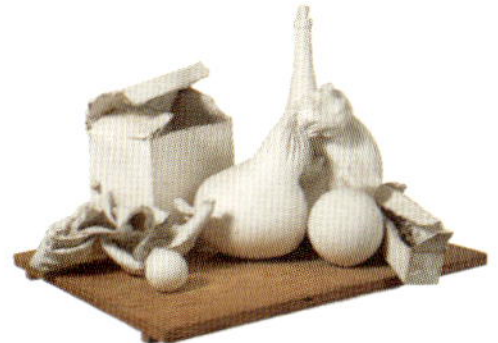

Still Life #1, 1964
Hydrocal
15 x 23 x 22 in. (38.1 x 58.4 x 55.8 cm.)
Purchased from Richard Gray Gallery, Chicago, Illinois, 1970
Promised Gift of Natalie and Irving Forman

JOSEF ALBERS

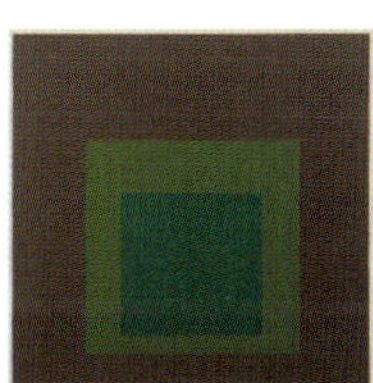

Homage to the Square: Unexpected, 1961
Oil on canvas mounted on board
30 x 30 in. (76.2 x 76.2 cm.)
Purchased from B.C. Holland Gallery, Chicago, Illinois, 1965
Collection Albright-Knox Art Gallery
Gift of Natalie and Irving Forman, 2004

TIMOTHY APP

Autumnal Light, 1980
Oil on canvas
40½ x 32⅛ in. (102.8 x 81.5 cm.)
Gift of the artist to David Anderson; gift of David Anderson to the Formans, 1990
Promised Gift of Natalie and Irving Forman

STUART ARENDS

Celadon 10, 1989
Latex and wax on fiberboard
48 x 48 x 6 in. (121.9 x 121.9 x 15.2 cm.)
Purchased from the artist, 1994
Promised Gift of Natalie and Irving Forman

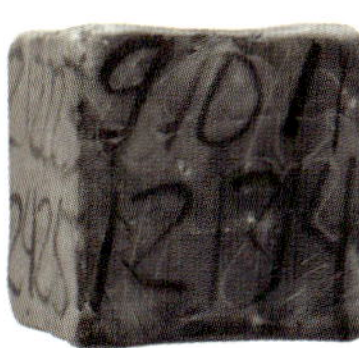

C.W.8, 1992
Oil and wax on wood
3⅝ x 3⅝ x 3½ in. (9.2 x 9.2 x 8.8 cm.)
Purchased from the artist, 1993
Promised Gift of Natalie and Irving Forman

O.S. 30, 1993
Oil on steel
3½ x 3½ x 3¼ in. (8.8 x 8.8 x 8.2 cm.)
Purchased from the artist, 1994
Promised Gift of Natalie and Irving Forman

JOE BARNES

Not titled [4], 1995
Oil on canvas
68 x 72 in. (172.7 x 182.8 cm.)
Purchased from Charlotte Jackson Fine Art, Santa Fe, New Mexico, 1995
Promised Gift of Natalie and Irving Forman

Not titled [6], 1995
Oil on canvas
16 x 16 in. (40.6 x 40.6 cm.)
Purchased from Charlotte Jackson Fine Art, Santa Fe, New Mexico, 1995
Promised Gift of Natalie and Irving Forman

***Not titled*, 1997**
Acrylic on canvas
24 x 22½ in. (60.9 x 57.1 cm.)
Purchased from Charlotte Jackson Fine Art, Santa Fe, New Mexico, 1998
Promised Gift of Natalie and Irving Forman

***Not titled [chromium green oxide]*, 1997**
Acrylic on canvas
24 x 22½ in. (60.9 x 57.1 cm.)
Purchased from Charlotte Jackson Fine Art, Santa Fe, New Mexico, 1998
Promised Gift of Natalie and Irving Forman

JOHN BEECH

***Contact Glue Painting*, 1993**
Contact cement on particleboard
11⅜ x 11⅜ in. (28.9 x 28.9 cm.)
Purchased from Gallery Paule Anglim, San Francisco, California, 1996
Promised Gift of Natalie and Irving Forman

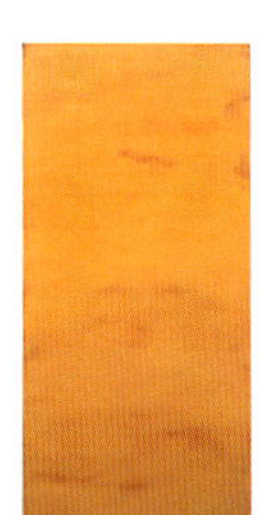

***Large Elmer Painting*, 1993–1995, 2000**
Glue and turmeric on fiberboard
77½ x 35 x 3 in. (196.8 x 88.9 x 7.6 cm.)
Purchased from Gallery Paule Anglim, San Francisco, California, 1996
Collection Albright-Knox Art Gallery
Gift of Natalie and Irving Forman, 2003

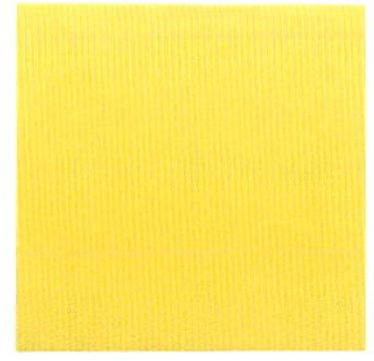

***Adhesive Painting*, 1996–2000**
Glue on wood
21 x 21 in. (53.3 x 53.3 cm.)
Purchased from Charlotte Jackson Fine Art, Santa Fe, New Mexico, 2002
Collection Albright-Knox Art Gallery
Gift of Natalie and Irving Forman, 2004

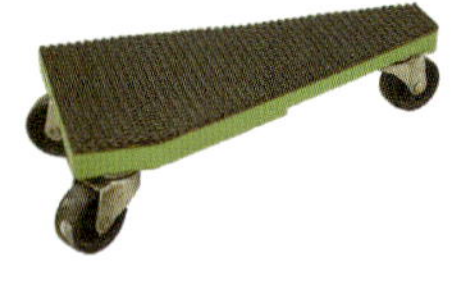

Not titled, 1998
Wood, casters, rubber, and enamel
3½ x 12½ x 6½ in. (8.8 x 31.7 x 16.5 cm.)
Gift of the artist to the Formans, ca. 1998
Promised Gift of Natalie and Irving Forman

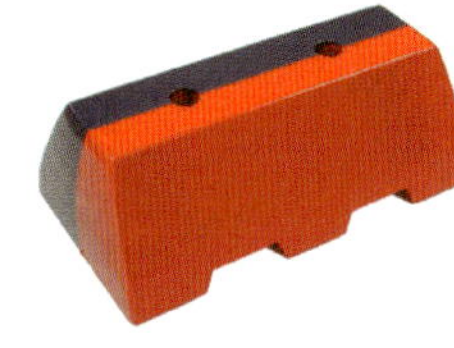

Small Bumper Edition (1/15), 1999
Enamel on wood
4½ x 12 x 6½ in. (11.4 x 30.4 x 16.5 cm.)
Gift of the artist to the Formans, ca. 2001
Promised Gift of Natalie and Irving Forman

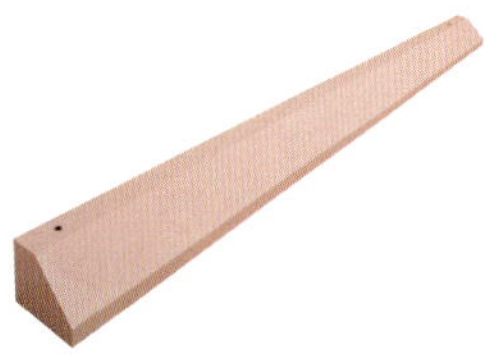

***Diminishing Bumper-Pink*, 2001**
Enamel on wood and metal pipe
8 x 98 x 11 in. (20.3 x 248.9 x 27.9 cm.)
Purchased from Charlotte Jackson Fine Art, Santa Fe, New Mexico, 2002
Collection Albright-Knox Art Gallery
Gift of Natalie and Irving Forman, 2004

Rotating Painting #78, 2001
Enamel on Plexiglas mounted on wood and steel
5 x 6 x 11 in. (12.7 x 15.2 x 27.9 cm.)
Gift of the artist to the Formans, 2002
Promised Gift of Natalie and Irving Forman

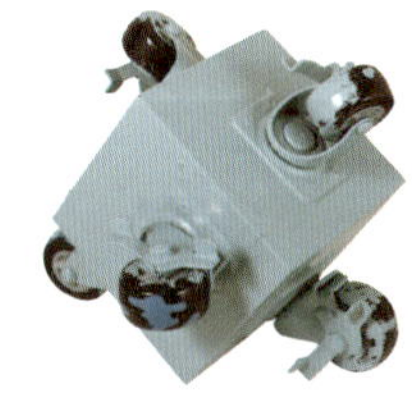

***Small Rolling Platform #49*, 2001**
Enamel on wood and casters
10 x 10 x 10 in. (25.4 x 25.4 x 25.4 cm.)
Purchased from Charlotte Jackson Fine Art, Santa Fe, New Mexico, 2002
Promised Gift of Natalie and Irving Forman

***Bent Glue Painting*, 2002**
Glue on canvas mounted on wood
8 x 7½ x 9 in. (20.3 x 19 x 22.8 cm.)
Purchased from Charlotte Jackson Fine Art, Santa Fe, New Mexico, 2002
Collection Albright-Knox Art Gallery
Gift of Natalie and Irving Forman, 2004

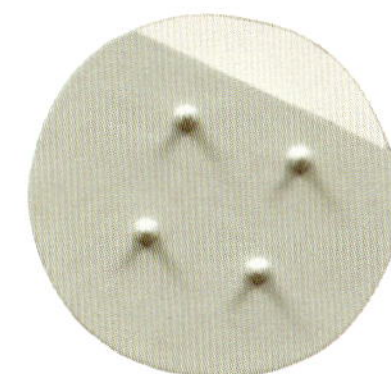

***Rotating Painting*, 2002**
Enamel on Plexiglas mounted on wood
8-in. diameter x 2½ in. (20.3-cm diameter x 6.3 cm.)
Gift of the artist to the Formans, 2002
Promised Gift of Natalie and Irving Forman

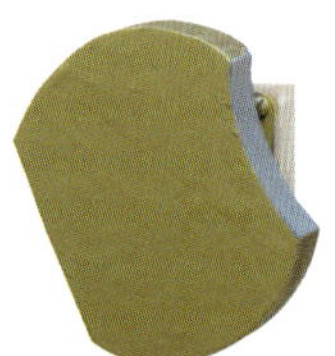

RP #156, 2003
Enamel on Plexiglas mounted on wood
5 x 3⅝ x 2½ in. (12.7 x 9.2 x 6.3 cm.)
Gift of the artist to the Formans, 2004
Promised Gift of Natalie and Irving Forman

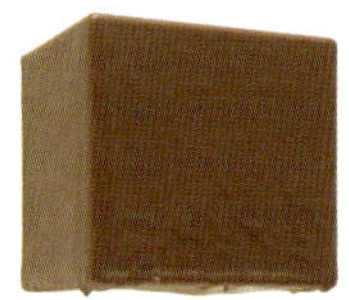

Glue Painting #59, **2004**
Glue on wood
4 x 4¾ x 4 in. (10.1 x 12 x 10.1 cm.)
Purchased from the artist through Charlotte Jackson Fine Art, Santa Fe, New Mexico, 2004
Promised Gift of Natalie and Irving Forman

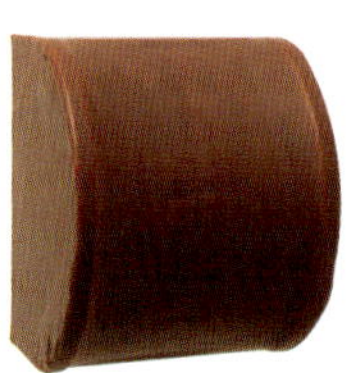

Glue Painting #64, **2004**
Glue on wood
9¾ x 7¾ x 7⅞ in. (24.7 x 19.6 x 20 cm.)
Purchased from the artist through Charlotte Jackson Fine Art, Santa Fe, New Mexico, 2004
Promised Gift of Natalie and Irving Forman

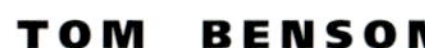

TOM BENSON

Ability, 2000
Oil on aluminum and acrylic sheet
17¼ x 12¼ in. (43.8 x 31.1 cm.)
Purchased from Charlotte Jackson Fine Art, Santa Fe, New Mexico, 2000
Promised Gift of Natalie and Irving Forman

Future, **2000**
Oil on aluminum
23⅝ x 24¼ in. (60 x 61.5 cm.)
Purchased from Charlotte Jackson Fine Art, Santa Fe, New Mexico, 2000
Promised Gift of Natalie and Irving Forman

ERIKA BLUMENFELD

Aqua Blue/Light Green, **2003**
Automotive paint on Z-type aluminum
19¼ x 23¼ in. (48.8 x 59 cm.)
Purchased from Charlotte Jackson Fine Art, Santa Fe, New Mexico, 2003
Promised Gift of Natalie and Irving Forman

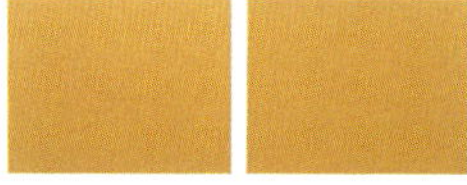

Untitled (Yellow/Light Gold), **2003**
Automotive paint on aluminum
Diptych, 7½ x 9½ in. (19 x 24.1 cm.) each; 7½ x 19⅜ in. (19 x 49.2 cm.) overall
Gift of the artist to the Formans, 2004
Promised Gift of Natalie and Irving Forman

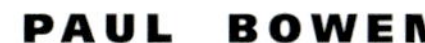

PAUL BOWEN

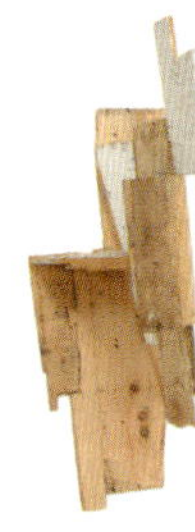

Free Fall, 1994
Wood and mixed media
32 x 12 x 9 in. (81.2 x 30.4 x 22.8 cm.)
Purchased from Jack Shainman Gallery, New York, New York, 1994
Promised Gift of Natalie and Irving Forman

MALA BREUER

Not titled, **1993**
Oil on canvas
12 x 12 in. (30. 4 x 30.4 cm.)
Purchased from Charlotte Jackson Fine Art, Santa Fe, New Mexico, 1993
Promised Gift of Natalie and Irving Forman

Not titled, 1993
Oil on canvas
12 x 12 in. (30.4 x 30.4 cm.)
Gift of the artist to the Formans
Promised Gift of Natalie and Irving Forman

RODNEY CARSWELL

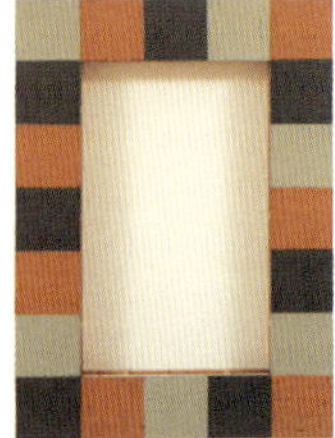

Two Grays and Orange Around an Empty Rectangle, 1988
Oil and wax on canvas
66 x 48 x 4 in. (167.6 x 121.9 x 10.1 cm.)
Purchased from Linda Durham Gallery, Santa Fe, New Mexico, 1990
Promised Gift of Natalie and Irving Forman

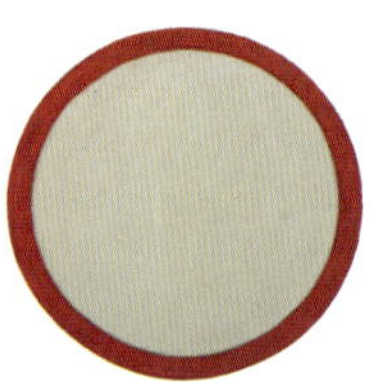

Red Circle / White Center, 1991
Oil and wax on wood
18 ¼-in. diameter x 3 ¼ in.
(45.7-cm. diameter x 8.2 cm.)
Purchased from Charlotte Jackson Fine Art, Santa Fe, New Mexico, 1994
Collection Albright-Knox Art Gallery
Gift of Natalie and Irving Forman, 2003

JOHN CHAMBERLAIN

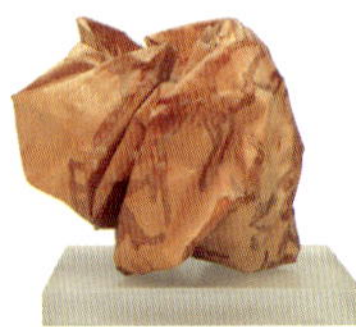

Penthouse #69, 1969
Paper bag, resin, and watercolor
8 x 8 x 7 in. (20.3 x 20.3 x 17.7 cm.)
Purchased from Lo Giudice Gallery, Chicago, Illinois, 1984
Promised Gift of Natalie and Irving Forman

MARK COLE

Not titled, 2002
Polyurethane cast
28 x 30 in. (71.1 x 76.2 cm.)
Selected at the artist's studio by John Beech for purchase by the Formans, 2002
Promised Gift of Natalie and Irving Forman

JOHN CONNELL

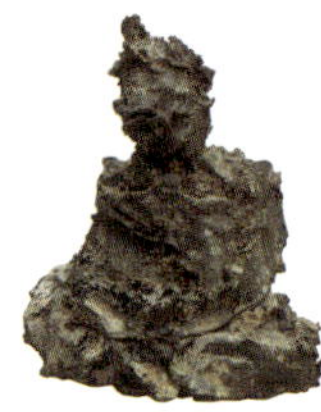

Not titled, CA. 1985
Bronze
10 x 6 x 4 in. (25.4 x 15.2 x 10.1 cm.)
Purchased from Linda Durham Gallery, Santa Fe, New Mexico, 1989
Promised Gift of Natalie and Irving Forman

RUDOLF DE CRIGNIS

Painting #96.9, 1996
Oil on canvas
30 x 30 in. (76.2 x 76.2 cm.)
Purchased from Charlotte Jackson Fine Art, Santa Fe, New Mexico, 1996
Promised Gift of Natalie and Irving Forman

Painting #98.7, 1998
Oil on canvas
60 x 60 in. (152.4 x 152.4 cm.)
Purchased from Charlotte Jackson Fine Art, Santa Fe, New Mexico, 1998
Collection Albright-Knox Art Gallery
Gift of Natalie and Irving Forman, 2003

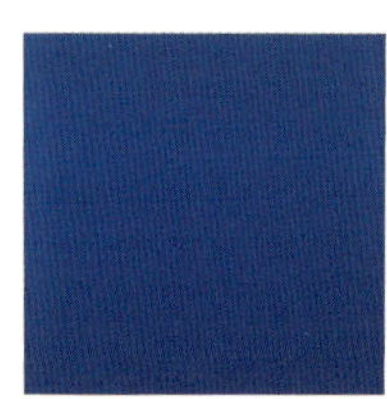

Painting #01-37, 2001
Oil on canvas
60 x 60 in. (152.4 x 152.4 cm.)
Purchased from Charlotte Jackson Fine Art, Santa Fe, New Mexico, 2002
Promised Gift of Natalie and Irving Forman

CONSTANCE DEJONG

Square IV, 1992
Paint on copper
36 x 36 in. (91.4 x 91.4 cm.)
Purchased from Linda Durham Gallery, Santa Fe, New Mexico, 1993
Collection Albright-Knox Art Gallery
Gift of Natalie and Irving Forman, 2004

BURGOYNE DILLER

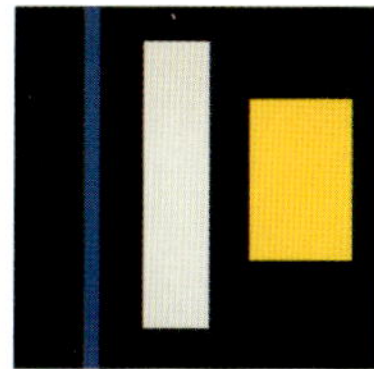

First Theme #35, 1955-1960
Oil on canvas
42 x 42 in. (106.6 x 106.6 cm.)
Purchased from Galerie Chalette, New York, New York, 1965
Collection Albright-Knox Art Gallery
Gift of Natalie and Irving Forman, 2004

MARK DI SUVERO

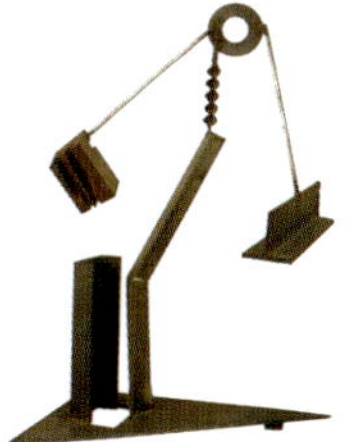

Untitled, 1967
Steel
29 ¼ x 26 x 17 in. (74.2 x 66 x 43.1 cm.)
Purchased from Richard Bellamy Gallery, New York, New York, 1967
Promised Gift of Natalie and Irving Forman

ALAN EBNOTHER

Abhor, 1995
Oil on linen
28 x 28 in. (71.1 x 71.1 cm.)
Purchased from Charlotte Jackson Fine Art, Santa Fe, New Mexico, 1995
Promised Gift of Natalie and Irving Forman

Abjects, 1996
Oil on linen
36 x 36 in. (91.4 x 91.4 cm.)
Purchased from Charlotte Jackson Fine Art, Santa Fe, New Mexico, 1996
Promised Gift of Natalie and Irving Forman

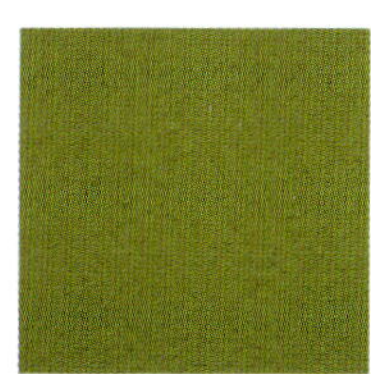

Able, 1996
Oil on linen
36 x 36 in. (91.4 x 91.4 cm.)
Purchased from Charlotte Jackson Fine Art, Santa Fe, New Mexico, 1996
Promised Gift of Natalie and Irving Forman

Abomination, 1996
Oil on linen
62 x 59 in. (157.4 x 149.8 cm.)
Purchased from Charlotte Jackson Fine Art, Santa Fe, New Mexico, 1997
Promised Gift of Natalie and Irving Forman

Accord, 1997
Oil on copper mounted on wood
12 ¾ x 10 ¼ in. (32.3 x 26 cm.)
Purchased from Charlotte Jackson Fine Art, Santa Fe, New Mexico, 1997
Promised Gift of Natalie and Irving Forman

Adorn, 1997
Oil on linen
41 x 39 in. (104.1 x 99 cm.)
Gift of the artist to the Formans, 1997
Promised Gift of Natalie and Irving Forman

Agony, 1998
Oil on linen
48 x 44 in. (121.9 x 111.7 cm.)
Purchased from Charlotte Jackson Fine Art, Santa Fe, New Mexico, 1998
Promised Gift of Natalie and Irving Forman

Alarm, 1998
Oil on linen
31 ¼ x 29 ½ in. (79.3 x 74.9 cm.)
Purchased from the artist, 2002
Collection Albright-Knox Art Gallery
Gift of Natalie and Irving Forman, 2003

Allure, 1999
Oil on linen
39 x 39 in. (99 x 99 cm.)
Gift of the artist to the Formans, 1999
Promised Gift of Natalie and Irving Forman

Angry, 2000
Oil on linen
59 x 57 in. (149.8 x 144.7 cm.)
Purchased from Charlotte Jackson Fine Art, Santa Fe, New Mexico, 2001
Promised Gift of Natalie and Irving Forman

#4, 2001
Oil on aluminum
4 x 4 in. (10.1 x 10.1 cm.)
Gift of the artist to the Formans, 2001
Promised Gift of Natalie and Irving Forman

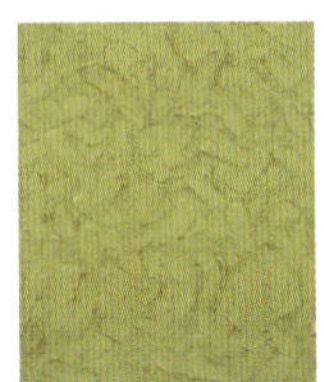

April 1, 2003, 2003
Oil on linen
19¾ x 15¾ in. (50.1 x 40 cm.)
Gift of the artist to the Formans, 2003
Promised Gift of Natalie and Irving Forman

ALLAN GRAHAM

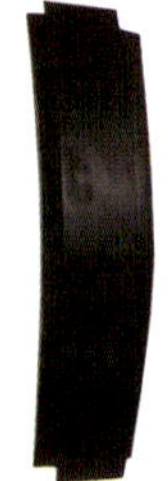

Hinge, 1987
Oil and wax on linen
96 x 27 x 6½ in. (243.8 x 68.5 x 16.5 cm.)
Purchased from the artist, 1989
Promised Gift of Natalie and Irving Forman

GLORIA GRAHAM

FeS2 Pyrite, 1997
Watercolor and kaolin with wax on cotton mounted on wood
14 x 14 in. (35.5 x 35.5 cm.)
Purchased from Kathleen Shields Contemporary Art Projects, Albuquerque, New Mexico, 1997
Collection Albright-Knox Art Gallery
Gift of Natalie and Irving Forman, 2003

MARCIA HAFIF

Roman Painting XXVII, 1988
Oil over acrylic on linen
13 x 12 in. (33 x 30.4 cm.)
Purchased from Charlotte Jackson Fine Art, Santa Fe, New Mexico, 1997
Promised Gift of Natalie and Irving Forman

French Painting: Terraile, 1990
Oil on cotton
60 x 60 in. (152.4 x 152.4 cm.)
Purchased from Charlotte Jackson Fine Art, Santa Fe, New Mexico, 1997
Promised Gift of Natalie and Irving Forman

Red Painting: Indian Yellow Tint, 1998
Oil on cotton
58 x 58 in. (147.3 x 147.3 cm.)
Purchased from Charlotte Jackson Fine Art, Santa Fe, New Mexico, 1998
Promised Gift of Natalie and Irving Forman

Red Painting: Paliogen Maroon, 1998
Oil on cotton
58 x 58 in. (147.3 x 147.3 cm.)
Purchased from Charlotte Jackson Fine Art, Santa Fe, New Mexico, 1998
Collection Albright-Knox Art Gallery
Gift of Natalie and Irving Forman, 2003

JAMES HAYWARD

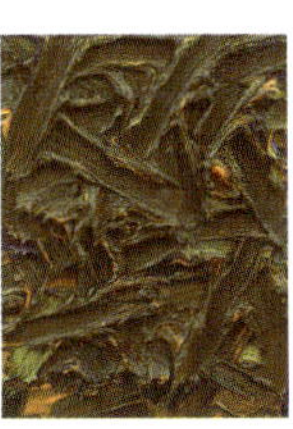

Chromachord #47, 1999
Oil on canvas mounted on board
13½ x 10½ in. (34.2 x 26.7 cm.)
Purchased from Charlotte Jackson Fine Art, Santa Fe, New Mexico, 1999
Promised Gift of Natalie and Irving Forman

Chromachord #49, 1999
Oil on canvas mounted on board
13½ x 10½ in. (34.2 x 26.7 cm.)
Purchased from Charlotte Jackson Fine Art, Santa Fe, New Mexico, 1999
Promised Gift of Natalie and Irving Forman

JAMES HOWELL

Clay Series No. 1 and _Clay Series No. 2_ (units 1 & 2 of 9), 1992
Acrylic on aluminum
Diptych, 18 x 18 in. (45.7 x 45.7 cm.) each; 18 x 38 in. (45.7 x 96.5 cm.) overall
Purchased from Charlotte Jackson Fine Art, Santa Fe, New Mexico, 1994
Collection Albright-Knox Art Gallery
Gift of Natalie and Irving Forman, 2004

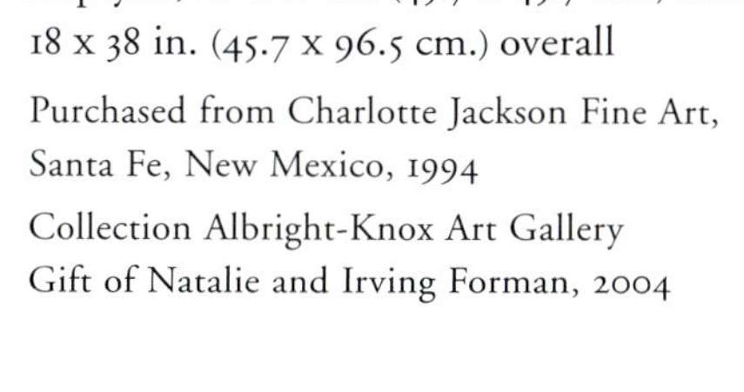

Light Stone Veil, 1992
Acrylic on aluminum
48 x 48 in. (121.9 x 121.9 cm.)
Purchased from Charlotte Jackson Fine Art, Santa Fe, New Mexico, 1995
Promised Gift of Natalie and Irving Forman

San Juan Series No. 6 and _San Juan Series No. 7_ (units 6 & 7 of 10), 1993
Acrylic on aluminum
Diptych, 18 x 18 in. (45.7 x 45.7 cm.) each; 18 x 38 in. (45.7 x 96.5 cm.) overall
Purchased from Charlotte Jackson Fine Art, Santa Fe, New Mexico, 1994
Collection Albright-Knox Art Gallery
Gift of Natalie and Irving Forman, 2003

(S1.9) Set 68.98 (unit 5 of 5), 1995
Acrylic on aluminum
33 x 33 in. (83.8 x 83.8 cm.)
Purchased from Charlotte Jackson Fine Art, Santa Fe, New Mexico, 1995
Promised Gift of Natalie and Irving Forman

(S6.4) Set 93.02, 1995
Acrylic on cotton duck
60 x 60 in. (152.4 x 152.4 cm.)
Purchased from Charlotte Jackson Fine Art, Santa Fe, New Mexico, 1995
Promised Gift of Natalie and Irving Forman

Dark Suite Four Part Painting, 2000–2001
A. *61.14*, dated 4/21/01; B. *57.04*, dated 3/18/01
C. *52.71*, dated 2/08/01; D. *48.17*, dated 2/19/00
Acrylic on canvas
15½ x 15½ in. (39.3 x 39.3 cm.) each; 15½ x 92 in. (39.3 x 233.6 cm.) overall
Purchased from Charlotte Jackson Fine Art, Santa Fe, New Mexico, 2002
Promised Gift of Natalie and Irving Forman

JAMES HYDE

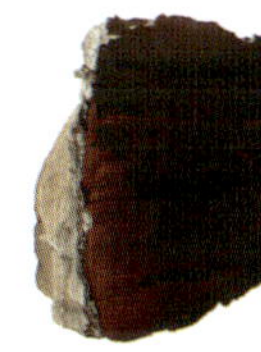

Part, 1993
Fresco on Styrofoam
9¼ x 10 x 5 in. (23.4 x 25.4 x 12.7 cm.)
Purchased from Charlotte Jackson Fine Art, Santa Fe, New Mexico, 1994
Promised Gift of Natalie and Irving Forman

RACHEL LACHOWICZ

Not titled, 2003
Lipstick on canvas
26 x 20 in. (66 x 50.8 cm.)
Substitute in 2003 for work originally purchased in 1992 from Rhona Hoffman Gallery, Chicago, Illinois
Collection Albright-Knox Art Gallery
Gift of Natalie and Irving Forman, 2003

JODY LOMBERG

Slip 11, 1993
Mixed media on canvas
36 x 50 in. (91.4 x 127 cm.)
Purchased from Jack Shainman Gallery, New York, New York, 1994
Promised Gift of Natalie and Irving Forman

ED MALINA

103B, 1991
Acrylic on wood
19 x 23 in. (48.2 x 58.4 cm.)
Purchased from the artist, 1992
Promised Gift of Natalie and Irving Forman

103W, 1991
Acrylic on wood
19 x 20 in. (48.2 x 50.8 cm.)
Purchased from the artist, 1993
Promised Gift of Natalie and Irving Forman

242B, 1992
Acrylic on wood
20 x 20 in. (50.8 x 50.8 cm.)
Purchased from the artist, 1993
Promised Gift of Natalie and Irving Forman

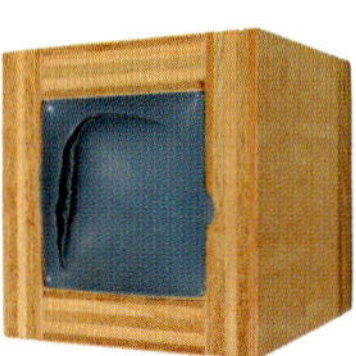

Untitled, N.D.
Acrylic and wood
4 x 4 x 4 in. (10.1 x 10.1 x 10.1 cm.)
Gift of the artist to the Formans, 1997
Promised Gift of Natalie and Irving Forman

JOSEPH MARIONI

Red Painting, 1995
Acrylic on linen
79 x 76 in. (200.6 x 193 cm.)
Purchased from Charlotte Jackson Fine Art, Santa Fe, New Mexico, 1996
Collection Albright-Knox Art Gallery
Gift of Natalie and Irving Forman, 2003

Green Painting, 1996
Acrylic on linen
71½ x 68 in. (181.6 x 172.7 cm.)
Purchased from Charlotte Jackson Fine Art, Santa Fe, New Mexico, 1996
Promised Gift of Natalie and Irving Forman

Blue Painting, 1997
Acrylic on linen
24 x 23 in. (60.9 x 58.4 cm.)
Purchased from Charlotte Jackson Fine Art, Santa Fe, New Mexico, 1997
Promised Gift of Natalie and Irving Forman

White Painting, 1997
Acrylic on linen
55 x 51 in. (139.7 x 129.5 cm.)
Purchased from Charlotte Jackson Fine Art, Santa Fe, New Mexico, 1998
Promised Gift of Natalie and Irving Forman

Yellow Painting, 1997
Acrylic on linen
79 x 74 in. (200.6 x 187.9 cm.)
Purchased from Charlotte Jackson Fine Art, Santa Fe, New Mexico, 1998
Promised Gift of Natalie and Irving Forman

ALLAN McCOLLUM

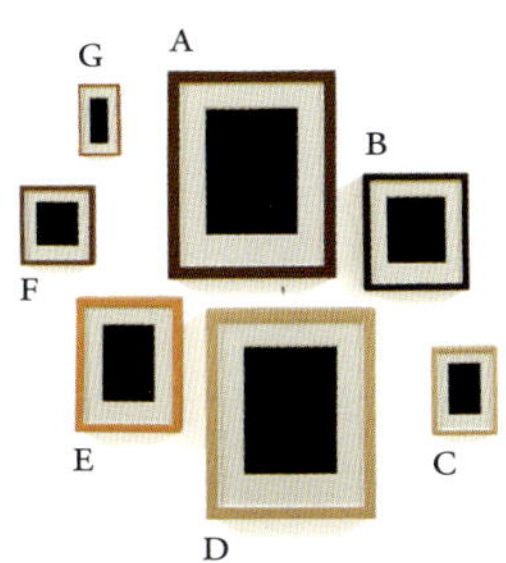

***Surrogates Paintings,* 1983**
Acrylic on plaster
A. *#19-1-1983*, 20 x 16 in. (50.8 x 40.6 cm.)
B. *#4-10-1983*, 11¾ x 10 in. (29.8 x 25.4 cm.)
C. *#8-15-1983*, 8½ x 6¼ in. (21.5 x 15.8 cm.)
D. *#8-1-1983*, 20 x 16 in. (50.8 x 40.6 cm.)
E. *#5-7-1983*, 13 x 10 in. (33 x 25.4 cm.)
F. *#21-16-1983*, 7¾ x 7¼ in. (19.6 x 18.4 cm.)
G. *#7-17-1983*, 7 x 4 in. (17.7 x 10.1 cm.)

Purchased from Rhona Hoffman Gallery, Chicago, Illinois, 1983

Promised Gift of Natalie and Irving Forman

JOHN MEYER

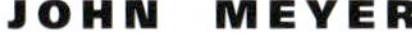

Not titled, 1986
Industrial lacquer on wood
5 15/16 x 5 15/16 in. (15 x 15 cm.)

Gift of the artist to Alan Ebnother; gift of Alan Ebnother to his daughter Jamie; gift of Jamie Ebnother to the Formans, 2004

Promised Gift of Natalie and Irving Forman

***Not titled,* CA. 1989**
Oil on linen
65 x 64½ in. (165.1 x 163.8 cm.)

Purchased from Angles Gallery, Santa Monica, California, 1996

Promised Gift of Natalie and Irving Forman

***Not titled,* 1991**
Oil on linen
36 x 36 in. (91.4 x 91.4 cm.)

Purchased from Mincher/Wilcox Gallery, San Francisco, California, 1994

Promised Gift of Natalie and Irving Forman

***Not titled,* 1993–1995**
Egg tempera, gesso, and linen mounted on oak panel
Diptych, 72 x 72 x 5 in. (182.8 x 182.8 x 12.7 cm.) each; 72 x 148 x 5 in. (182.8 x 375.9 x 12.7 cm.) overall

Purchased from Gallery Paule Anglim, San Francisco, California, 1995

Promised Gift of Natalie and Irving Forman

***Not titled,* 1994**
Tempera on mahogany panel
Diptych, 18½ x 18½ in. (46.9 x 46.9 cm.) each; 18½ x 37 in. (46.9 x 93.9 cm.) overall

Purchased from Gallery Paule Anglim, San Francisco, California, 1995

Promised Gift of Natalie and Irving Forman

Not titled, 1994
Egg tempera on board
15¼ x 15¼ in. (38.7 x 38.7 cm.)

Gift of the artist to the Formans, 1995

Promised Gift of Natalie and Irving Forman

***Not titled,* 1996**
Egg tempera on walnut panel
Diptych, 20 x 20 in. (50.8 x 50.8 cm.) each; 20 x 41 in. (50.8 x 104.1 cm.) overall

Purchased from Charlotte Jackson Fine Art, Santa Fe, New Mexico, 1996

Promised Gift of Natalie and Irving Forman

Not titled, 1996
Oil on fiberboard
Diptych, 24 x 24 in. (60.9 x 60.9 cm.) each; 24 x 48 in. (60.9 x 121.9 cm.) overall

Gift of the artist to the Formans, 1996

Promised Gift of Natalie and Irving Forman

Not titled, 1997
Egg tempera on plywood
Diptych, 5 x 5 in. (12.7 x 12.7 cm.) each;
5 x 10 in. (12.7 x 25.4 cm.) overall
Gift of the artist to the Formans, 1997
Promised Gift of Natalie and Irving Forman

***Not titled,* 1997**
Egg tempera on wood
Diptych, 24 x 24 in. (60.9 x 60.9 cm.) each;
24 x 49 in. (60.9 x 124.4 cm.) overall
Purchased from Charlotte Jackson Fine Art,
Santa Fe, New Mexico, 1997
Collection Albright-Knox Art Gallery
Gift of Natalie and Irving Forman, 2003

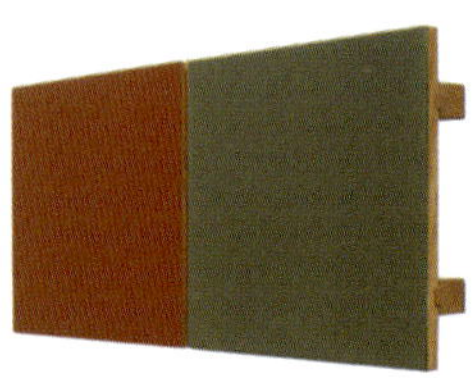

Not titled, 1998
Egg tempera on oak panel
Diptych, 9¾ x 9¾ in. (24.7 x 24.7 cm.) each;
9¾ x 19¾ in. (24.7 x 50.1 cm.) overall
Gift of the artist to the Formans, 1998
Promised Gift of Natalie and Irving Forman

***Not titled,* 2000**
Ground lapis and ground malachite with
egg tempera on white oak panel
Diptych, 10 x 10 in. (25.4 x 25.4 cm.) each;
10 x 20 in. (25.4 x 50.8 cm.) overall
Purchased from Charlotte Jackson Fine Art,
Santa Fe, New Mexico, 2000
Promised Gift of Natalie and Irving Forman

Not titled, 2001
Egg tempera and lapis lazuli on coated Plexiglas
12 x 12 in. (30.4 x 30.4 cm.)
Gift of the artist to the Formans, 2001
Promised Gift of Natalie and Irving Forman

***Not titled,* 2001**
Tempera on walnut panel
17 x 19 in. (43.1 x 48.2 cm.)
Purchased from Charlotte Jackson Fine Art,
Santa Fe, New Mexico, 2001
Promised Gift of Natalie and Irving Forman

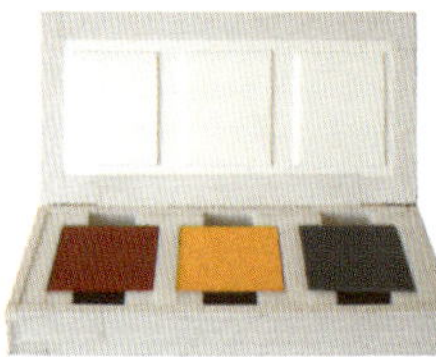

Not titled, 2002
Ground cinnabar, arsenic, and lapis lazuli with
egg tempera on wood in storage box [maquettes
for triptych purchased by Lannan Foundation]
Triptych, 4 x 4 x 4 in. (10.1 x 10.1 x 10.1 cm.) each
Gift of the artist to the Formans, 2002
Promised Gift of Natalie and Irving Forman

PATRICIA MOISAN

***Perforation,* 1995**
Pigment and resin on aluminum
20 x 20 in. (50.8 x 50.8 cm.)
Purchased from Angles Gallery, Santa Monica,
California, 1995
Promised Gift of Natalie and Irving Forman

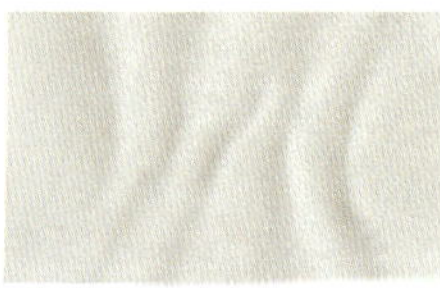

1624 Heads, 2002
Dried pigment on acrylic
17½ x 28½ in. (44.5 x 72.4 cm.)
Gift of the artist to the Formans, 2003
Promised Gift of Natalie and Irving Forman

DOUG OHLSON

***Sneaky-Pete,* 1965–1966**
Oil on canvas
Joined diptych, 24 x 48 in. (60.9 x 121.9 cm.)
Purchased from the artist, ca. 1966
Promised Gift of Natalie and Irving Forman

FLORENCE PIERCE

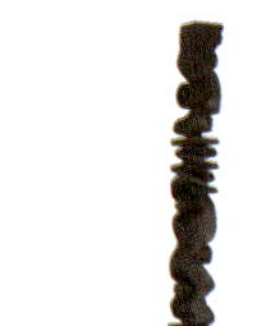
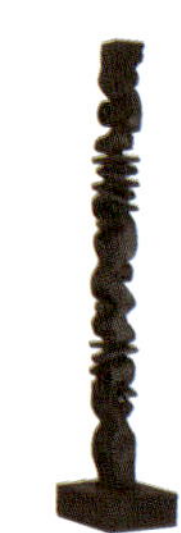

***Totem #6,* 1967**
Oil pigment on wood
52 x 7½ x 9½ in. 132 x 19 x 24.1 cm.)
Purchased from Charlotte Jackson Fine Art,
Santa Fe, New Mexico, 2002
Promised Gift of Natalie and Irving Forman

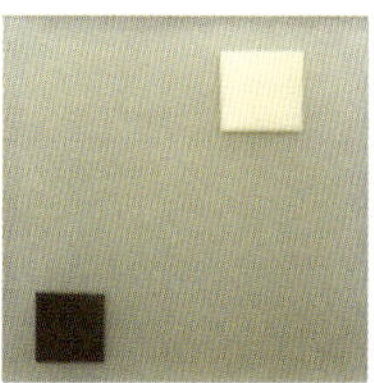

Untitled #43, 1992
Resin relief on mirrored Plexiglas
16 x 16 in. (40.6 x 40.6 cm.)
Purchased from Charlotte Jackson Fine Art, Santa Fe, New Mexico, 1992
Promised Gift of Natalie and Irving Forman

Untitled #86B, 1992
Resin relief on mirrored Plexiglas
16 x 16 in. (40.6 x 40.6 cm.)
Purchased from Center for Contemporary Art, Santa Fe, New Mexico, 1992
Promised Gift of Natalie and Irving Forman

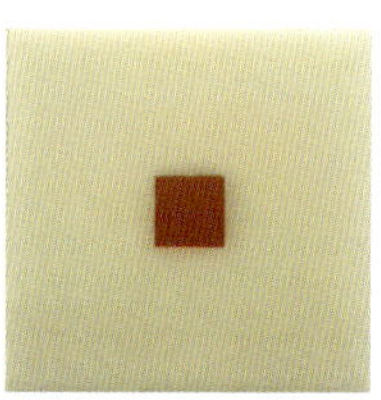

Untitled #118 (Red Square), 1993
Resin relief on mirrored Plexiglas
16 x 16 in. (40.6 x 40.6 cm.)
Purchased from Charlotte Jackson Fine Art, Santa Fe, New Mexico, 1993
Promised Gift of Natalie and Irving Forman

***Untitled #9,* 1994**
Resin relief on mirrored Plexiglas
24 x 24 in. (60.9 x 60.9 cm.)
Purchased from Rhona Hoffman Gallery, Chicago, Illinois, 1994
Promised Gift of Natalie and Irving Forman

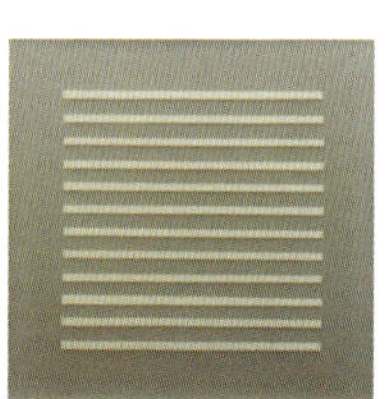

***Untitled #16,* 1994**
Resin relief on mirrored Plexiglas
24 x 24 in. (60.9 x 60.9 cm.)
Purchased from Charlotte Jackson Fine Art, Santa Fe, New Mexico, 1994
Promised Gift of Natalie and Irving Forman

Untitled #109, 1994
Resin relief on mirrored Plexiglas
32 x 32 in. (81.2 x 81.2 cm.)
Purchased from Charlotte Jackson Fine Art, Santa Fe, New Mexico, 1994
Promised Gift of Natalie and Irving Forman

***Untitled #117,* 1995**
Resin relief on mirrored Plexiglas
24 x 24 in. (60.9 x 60.9 cm.)
Purchased from Charlotte Jackson Fine Art, Santa Fe, New Mexico, 1995
Promised Gift of Natalie and Irving Forman

Untitled #118, 1995
Resin relief on mirrored Plexiglas
24 x 24 in. (60.9 x 60.9 cm.)
Purchased from Charlotte Jackson Fine Art, Santa Fe, New Mexico, 1995
Promised Gift of Natalie and Irving Forman

Untitled #134 (Pure Blue), 1996
Resin relief on mirrored Plexiglas
16 x 16 in. (40.6 x 40.6 cm.)
Gift of the artist to the Formans, 1996
Promised Gift of Natalie and Irving Forman

***Untitled #246 (Pink),* 1999**
Resin relief on mirrored Plexiglas
24 x 24 in. (60.9 x 60.9 cm.)
Purchased from Charlotte Jackson Fine Art, Santa Fe, New Mexico, 1999
Collection Albright-Knox Art Gallery
Gift of Natalie and Irving Forman, 2003

***Untitled #346,* 1999**
Resin relief on mirrored Plexiglas
24 x 24 in. (60.9 x 60.9 cm.)
Purchased from Charlotte Jackson Fine Art, Santa Fe, New Mexico, 1999
Collection Albright-Knox Art Gallery
Gift of Natalie and Irving Forman, 2003

***Untitled #598,* 2002**
Resin relief on mirrored Plexiglas
24 x 24 in. (60.9 x 60.9 cm.)
Purchased from Charlotte Jackson Fine Art, Santa Fe, New Mexico, 2003
Promised Gift of Natalie and Irving Forman

WINSTON ROETH

Luzerne, 1994
Tempera on fiberboard
32 x 32 in. (81.2 x 81.2 cm.)
Purchased from Charlotte Jackson Fine Art
Santa Fe, New Mexico, 1994
Collection Albright-Knox Art Gallery
Gift of Natalie and Irving Forman, 2004

Dark 3x4, 1995
Tempera on cotton duck mounted on panel
48 x 36 in. (121.9 x 91.4 cm.)
Purchased from the artist through Stark Gallery,
New York, New York, 1995
Promised Gift of Natalie and Irving Forman

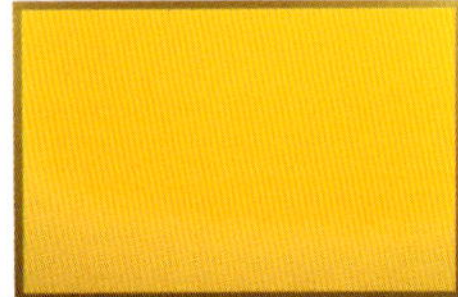

Dreamer, 2002
Tempera on panel
54 x 80 in. (137.1 x 203.2 cm.)
Purchased from Charlotte Jackson Fine Art,
Santa Fe, New Mexico, 2002
Collection Albright-Knox Art Gallery
Gift of Natalie and Irving Forman, 2003

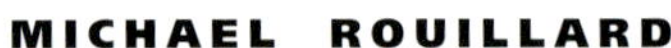

MICHAEL ROUILLARD

Not titled, 1994
Acrylic on Plexiglas
48 x 30 in. (121.9 x 76.2 cm.)
Purchased from Stark Gallery, New York,
New York, 1994
Promised Gift of Natalie and Irving Forman

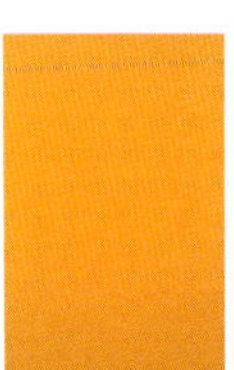

Not titled, 1994
Acrylic on Plexiglas
44½ x 28 in. (113 x 71.1 cm.)
Purchased from Stark Gallery, New York,
New York, 1994
Promised Gift of Natalie and Irving Forman

Trace, 2001
Acrylic on aluminum
Triptych, 50 x 30 in. (127 x 76.2 cm.) overall
Purchased from Charlotte Jackson Fine Art,
Santa Fe, New Mexico, 2002
Promised Gift of Natalie and Irving Forman

DAVID SIMPSON

Dark Iridescent Blue Green, 1990
Acrylic on canvas mounted on wood
12 x 12 in. (30.4 x 30.4 cm.)
Purchased from Charlotte Jackson Fine Art,
Santa Fe, New Mexico, 1995
Promised Gift of Natalie and Irving Forman

Silver Green, 1990
Acrylic on canvas mounted on wood
12 x 12 in. (30.4 x 30.4 cm.)
Purchased from Charlotte Jackson Fine Art,
Santa Fe, New Mexico, 1995
Promised Gift of Natalie and Irving Forman

New Primary (Blue), 1991
Acrylic on canvas mounted on wood
12 x 12 in. (30.4 x 30.4 cm.)
Purchased from Angles Gallery, Santa Monica,
California, 1994
Promised Gift of Natalie and Irving Forman

New Primary (Yellow), 1991
Acrylic on canvas mounted on wood
12 x 12 in. (30.4 x 30.4 cm.)
Purchased from Laura Carpenter Fine Art,
Santa Fe, New Mexico, 1995
Promised Gift of Natalie and Irving Forman

***Gold Over Green,* 1992**
Acrylic on canvas mounted on wood
12 x 12 in. (30.4 x 30.4 cm.)
Purchased from Angles Gallery, Santa Monica, California, 1994
Promised Gift of Natalie and Irving Forman

***Study: Yellow Violet Shift,* 1992–1994**
Acrylic on canvas mounted on wood
12 x 12 in. (30.4 x 30.4 cm.)
Purchased from Charlotte Jackson Fine Art, Santa Fe, New Mexico, 1995
Promised Gift of Natalie and Irving Forman

Golden Rectangle #8 (Golden Mean), 1992–1995
Acrylic on canvas mounted on wood
12 x 7½ in. (30.4 x 19 cm.)
Gift of the artist to the Formans, 1996
Promised Gift of Natalie and Irving Forman

***Interference Copper,* 1993**
Acrylic on canvas mounted on wood
12 x 12 in. (30.4 x 30.4 cm.)
Purchased from Laura Carpenter Fine Art, Santa Fe, New Mexico, 1995
Promised Gift of Natalie and Irving Forman

Burgundy, 1994
Acrylic on canvas
48 x 48 in. (121.9 x 121.9 cm.)
Purchased from Charlotte Jackson Fine Art, Santa Fe, New Mexico, 1995
Promised Gift of Natalie and Irving Forman

Port Royal, 1994
Acrylic on canvas
48 x 48 in. (121.9 x 121.9 cm.)
Purchased from Charlotte Jackson Fine Art, Santa Fe, New Mexico, 1995
Promised Gift of Natalie and Irving Forman

***Sky High,* 1994**
Acrylic on canvas
86 x 72 in. (218.4 x 182.8 cm.)
Purchased from Angles Gallery, Santa Monica, California, 1994
Collection Albright-Knox Art Gallery
Gift of Natalie and Irving Forman, 2003

***Study: Blue Inversion,* 1994**
Acrylic on canvas mounted on wood
12 x 12 in. (30.4 x 30.4 cm.)
Purchased from Charlotte Jackson Fine Art, Santa Fe, New Mexico, 1995
Promised Gift of Natalie and Irving Forman

Little Shift, 1995
Acrylic on canvas mounted on wood
10 x 10 in. (25.4 x 25.4 cm.)
Gift of the artist to the Formans, 1996
Promised Gift of Natalie and Irving Forman

***Flash Point,* 1996–2003**
Acrylic on canvas mounted on wood
12 x 12 in. (30.4 x 30.4 cm.)
Gift of the artist to the Formans, 2004
Promised Gift of Natalie and Irving Forman

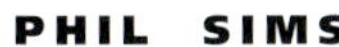

PHIL SIMS

***Pieve Caina #7 [cat. 166],* 1993**
Oil on linen mounted on wood
18 x 16 in. (45.7 x 40.6 cm.)
Purchased from Charlotte Jackson Fine Art, Santa Fe, New Mexico, 1998
Promised Gift of Natalie and Irving Forman

Not titled [cat. 228], 1995
Oil on linen
28 x 25 in. (71.1 x 63.5 cm.)
Purchased from Charlotte Jackson Fine Art, Santa Fe, New Mexico, 1998
Promised Gift of Natalie and Irving Forman

Not titled [cat. 343], 1998
Oil on linen
60 x 50 in. (152.4 x 127 cm.)
Purchased from Charlotte Jackson Fine Art, Santa Fe, New Mexico, 1998
Promised Gift of Natalie and Irving Forman

***Not titled [cat. 379]*, 1999**
Oil on linen
38 x 28 in. (96.5 x 71.1 cm.)
Purchased from Charlotte Jackson Fine Art, Santa Fe, New Mexico, 1999
Promised Gift of Natalie and Irving Forman

LEON POLK SMITH

First-One, 1954
Oil on cotton duck
39½-in. diameter (100.3-cm. diameter)
Purchased from B.C. Holland Gallery, Chicago, Illinois, 1964
Collection Albright-Knox Art Gallery
Gift of Natalie and Irving Forman, 2004

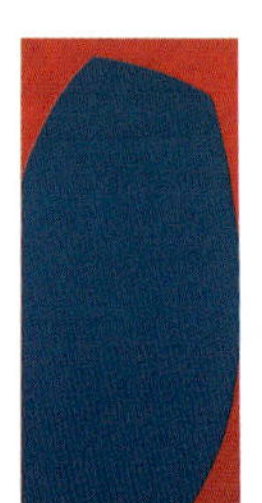

***Outer Rim*, 1962**
Oil on canvas
68 x 31 in. (172.7 x 78.7 cm.)
Purchased from B.C. Holland Gallery, Chicago, Illinois, 1964
Promised Gift of Natalie and Irving Forman

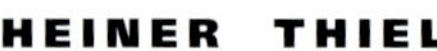

HEINER THIEL

MIV/94, #7/9, 1994
Graphite on steel
15¾ x 15¾ in. (40 x 40 cm.)
Purchased from Charlotte Jackson Fine Art, Santa Fe, New Mexico, 1997
Promised Gift of Natalie and Irving Forman

***MV/94, e.a., Nr. 2*, 1994**
Graphite on steel
15¾ x 15¾ in. (40 x 40 cm.)
Purchased from Charlotte Jackson Fine Art, Santa Fe, New Mexico, 1997
Promised Gift of Natalie and Irving Forman

***Untitled (Sphere, r=6.6ft.)*, 1998**
Anodized aluminum
38½ x 38½ x 4½ in. (97.7 x 97.7 x 11.4 cm.)
Purchased from Charlotte Jackson Fine Art, Santa Fe, New Mexico, 1998
Promised Gift of Natalie and Irving Forman

ROY THURSTON

93-4, 1993
Lacquer on wood
60 5/16 x 30 9/16 in. (153.1 x 77.6 cm.)
Purchased from Charlotte Jackson Fine Art, Santa Fe, New Mexico, 1997
Promised Gift of Natalie and Irving Forman

94-1, 1994
Lacquer on composite panel
Diptych, 30⅜ x 32½ in. (77.1 x 82.5 cm) each; 30⅜ x 78 in. (77.1 x 198.1 cm.) overall
Purchased from Angles Gallery, Santa Monica, California, 1994
Promised Gift of Natalie and Irving Forman

2001-5, 2001
Acrylic polyurethane on aluminum
20⅝ x 2¼ in. (52.4 x 5.7 cm.)
Gift of the artist to the Formans, 2001
Promised Gift of Natalie and Irving Forman

2001-8, 2001
Acrylic polyurethane on aluminum
24 x 19¼ in. (60.9 x 48.8 cm.)
Purchased from Charlotte Jackson Fine Art, Santa Fe, New Mexico, 2001
Collection Albright-Knox Art Gallery
Gift of Natalie and Irving Forman, 2003

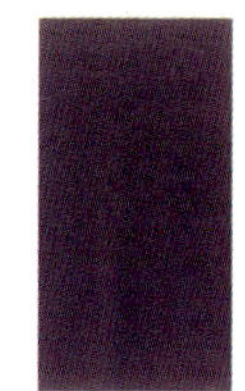

2001-16, 2001
Acrylic polyurethane on aluminum
23¾ x 12 5/16 in. (60.3 x 31.2 cm.)
Gift of the artist to the Formans, 2003
Promised Gift of Natalie and Irving Forman

2002-4, 2002
Acrylic polyurethane on aluminum
5⅝ x 4⅛ in. (14.2 x 10.4 cm.)
Gift from Charlotte Jackson, 2002
Promised Gift of Natalie and Irving Forman

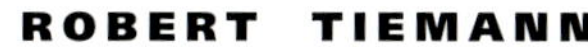

ROBERT TIEMANN

Not titled, 1979
Acrylic and cotton twine on canvas
61¼ x 61½ in. (155.5 x 156.2 cm.)
Purchased from Angles Gallery, Santa Monica, California, 1994
Collection Albright-Knox Art Gallery
Gift of Natalie and Irving Forman, 2003

Not titled, 1980
Acrylic and cotton twine on canvas
60 x 60¼ in. (152.4 x 153 cm.)
Purchased from Angles Gallery, Santa Monica, California, 1994
Promised Gift of Natalie and Irving Forman

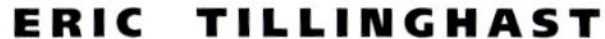

ERIC TILLINGHAST

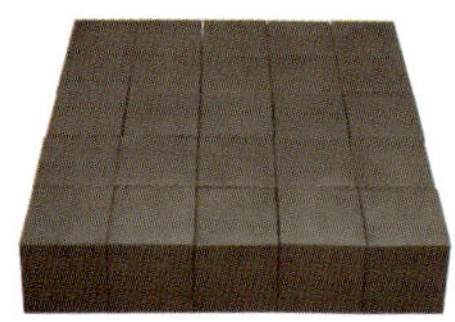

Not titled, 1996
Steel
7 x 30 x 30 in. (17.7 x 76.2 x 76.2 cm.)
Purchased from Charlotte Jackson Fine Art, Santa Fe, New Mexico, 2004
Promised Gift of Natalie and Irving Forman

#19G, 1998
Steel
48 x 37 in. (121.9 x 93.9 cm.)
Purchased from Charlotte Jackson Fine Art, Santa Fe, New Mexico, 1998
Promised Gift of Natalie and Irving Forman

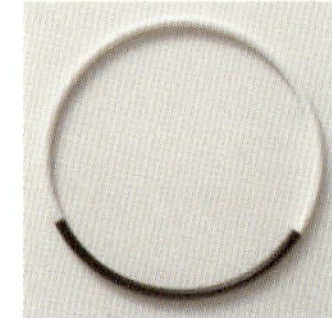

Ring #1, 2000
Paint on plastic
15½-in. diameter x ½ in.
(39.3-cm. diameter x 1.3 cm.)
Gift of the artist to the Formans, 2004
Promised Gift of Natalie and Irving Forman

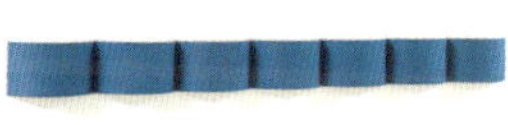

Aqua Fresh, 2003
Enamel on steel,
5 x 70 x 5 in. (12.7 x 177.8 x 12.7 cm.)
Purchased from Charlotte Jackson Fine Art, Santa Fe, New Mexico, 2003
Collection Albright-Knox Art Gallery
Gift of Natalie and Irving Forman, 2003

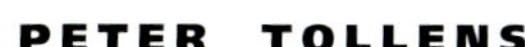

PETER TOLLENS

Not titled, 1992–1993
Egg tempera and oil on wood
12½ x 11¾ in. (31.7 x 29.8 cm.)
Purchased from Charlotte Jackson Fine Art, Santa Fe, New Mexico, 1997
Promised Gift of Natalie and Irving Forman

204, 1994–1996
Oil on wood
15 ¾ x 14 in. (40 x 35.5 cm.)
Purchased from Charlotte Jackson Fine Art, Santa Fe, New Mexico, 1997
Promised Gift of Natalie and Irving Forman

209, 1994–1996
Egg tempera and oil on wood
12 ⅛ x 11 in. (30.7 x 27.9 cm.)
Purchased from Charlotte Jackson Fine Art, Santa Fe, New Mexico, 1997
Promised Gift of Natalie and Irving Forman

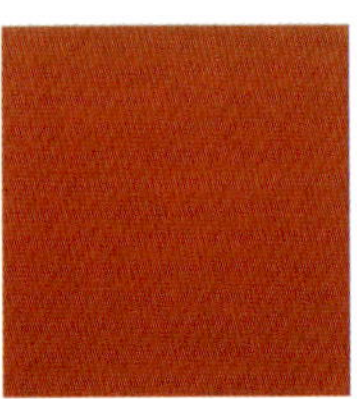

205, 1996
Egg tempera and oil on wood
20 x 18 ¼ in. (50.8 x 46.3 cm.)
Purchased from Charlotte Jackson Fine Art, Santa Fe, New Mexico, 1997
Promised Gift of Natalie and Irving Forman

218, 1996–1997
Egg tempera and oil on wood
33½ x 31 in. (85 x 78.7 cm.)
Purchased from Charlotte Jackson Fine Art, Santa Fe, New Mexico, 1997
Collection Albright-Knox Art Gallery
Gift of Natalie and Irving Forman, 2003

230, 1997
Egg tempera and oil on linen mounted on board
54½ x 34½ in. (138.4 x 87.6 cm.)
Purchased from Charlotte Jackson Fine Art, Santa Fe, New Mexico, 1998
Promised Gift of Natalie and Irving Forman

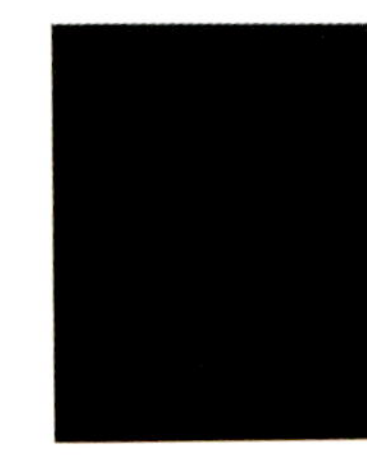

236, 1997
Egg tempera and oil on linen mounted on board
54½ x 42 in. (138.4 x 106.6 cm.)
Purchased from Charlotte Jackson Fine Art, Santa Fe, New Mexico, 1998
Promised Gift of Natalie and Irving Forman

271, 1997–1998
Egg tempera and oil on wood
27 x 25½ in. (68.5 x 64.7 cm.)
Purchased from Charlotte Jackson Fine Art, Santa Fe, New Mexico, 2002
Promised Gift of Natalie and Irving Forman

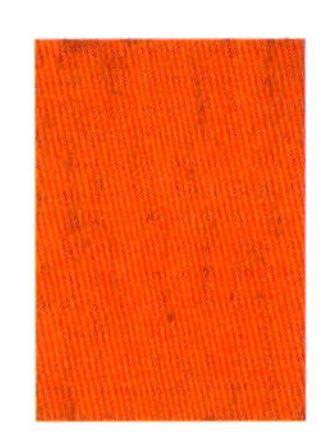

Not titled, 2001
Egg tempera and oil on wood
7 ¼ x 5 ¼ in. (18.4 x 13.3 cm.)
Gift of the artist to the Formans, 2001
Promised Gift of Natalie and Irving Forman

DIETER VILLINGER

Cadmium Orange, 1997
Oil on canvas mounted on board
16½ x 16½ in. (41.9 x 41.9 cm.)
Purchased from Charlotte Jackson Fine Art, Santa Fe, New Mexico, 1999
Promised Gift of Natalie and Irving Forman

Kobaltblau Hell Kobaltblau Turkis, 1998
Oil on canvas mounted on board
16½ x 16½ in. (41.9 x 41.9 cm.)
Purchased from Charlotte Jackson Fine Art, Santa Fe, New Mexico, 1999
Promised Gift of Natalie and Irving Forman

TOM WALDRON

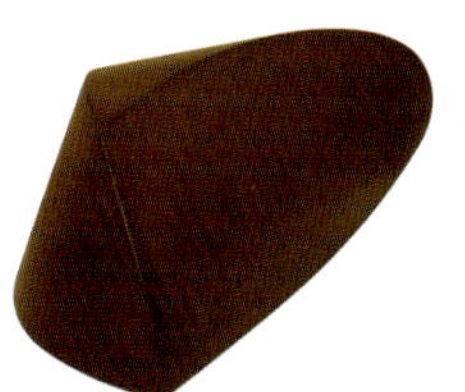

Untitled, 1997
Steel
8 x 18 x 9 in. (20.3 x 45.7 x 22.8 cm.)
Purchased from Conlon Siegel Gallery, Santa Fe, New Mexico, 1997
Promised Gift of Natalie and Irving Forman

ALAN WAYNE

#18, 1994
Oil and alkyd on canvas mounted on board
27 x 20½ in. (68.5 x 52 cm.)
Purchased from Newspace Gallery, Los Angeles, California, 1995
Promised Gift of Natalie and Irving Forman

#19, 1994
Oil and alkyd on canvas mounted on board
45 x 34 in. (114.3 x 86.3 cm.)
Purchased from Newspace Gallery, Los Angeles, California, 1998
Promised Gift of Natalie and Irving Forman

JOAN WITEK

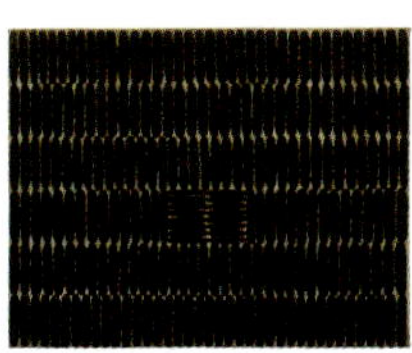

Not titled, 1980
Oil and graphite on canvas mounted on wood 24 x 30 in. (60.9 x 76.2 cm.)
Purchased from Rosa Esman Gallery, New York, New York, 1984
Collection Albright-Knox Art Gallery
Gift of Natalie and Irving Forman, 2003

PETER YOUNG

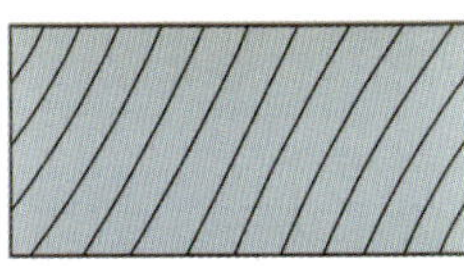

#2, 1968
Acrylic on canvas
54 x 108 in. (137.1 x 274.3 cm.)
From the artist to Richard Bellamy Gallery, New York; to Lo Giudice Gallery, Chicago; to Walter Kelly [Director of Lo Giudice Gallery]; purchased from Walter Kelly by the Formans, 1970
Promised Gift of Natalie and Irving Forman

INDEX

PHOTOGRAPHY CREDITS

All photographs are by James Hart unless otherwise noted below.

Robert Ryman, *State*, 1978, photograph courtesy Albright-Knox Art Gallery, P. 13.

Barnett Newman, *Vir Heroicus Sublimis*, 1950–1951, Digital Image © The Museum of Modern Art/Licensed by SCALA/Art Resource, New York; copyright © 2005 Barnett Newman Foundation / Artists Rights Society (ARS), New York, P. 15.

Kazimir Malevich, *Suprematist Composition: White on White*, 1918, digital image © The Museum of Modern Art / Licensed by SCALA/ Art Resource, New York, P. 17.

Yves Klein, *IKB 79*, 1959, Tate Gallery, London/Art Resource, New York; copyright © 2005 Artists Rights Society (ARS), New York / ADAGP, Paris, P. 19.

Ad Reinhardt, *Abstract Painting No. 5*, 1962, Tate Gallery, London/Art Resource, New York; copyright © 2005 Estate of Ad Reinhardt/Artists Rights Society (ARS), New York, P. 21.

Installation View, *Ellsworth Kelly: Chatham Series*, photograph courtesy Albright-Knox Art Gallery, P. 23.

Josef Albers, *Homage to the Square: Unexpected*, 1961, copyright © 2005 The Josef and Anni Albers Foundation/Artists Rights Society (ARS), New York, PP. 30, 165.

John Beech, *Not titled*, 1998, photograph by Erika Blumenfeld, P. 166.

John Beech, *Small Bumper Edition (1/15)*, 1999, photograph by Erika Blumenfeld, P. 166.

John Beech, *Rotating Painting #78*, 2001, photograph by Erika Blumenfeld, P. 166.

John Beech, *Rotating Painting*, 2002, photograph by Erika Blumenfeld, PP. 44, 166.

Erika Blumenfeld, *Aqua Blue/Light Green*, 2003, photograph by Erika Blumenfeld, PP. 49, 167.

Erika Blumenfeld, *Untitled (Yellow/Light Gold)*, 2003, photograph by Erika Blumenfeld, PP. 50, 167.

Paul Bowen, *Free Fall*, 1994, photograph by Erika Blumenfeld, P. 167.

John Chamberlain, *Penthouse #69*, 1969, photograph by Erika Blumenfeld, copyright © 2005 John Chamberlain /Artists Rights Society (ARS), New York, PP. 54, 168.

John Connell, *Not titled*, CA. 1985, photograph by Erika Blumenfeld, PP. 56, 168.

Burgoyne Diller, *First Theme #35*, 1955–1960, copyright Art © Estate of Burgoyne Diller/Licensed by VAGA, New York, New York/Est. Represented by the Michael Rosenfeld Gallery, PP. 61, 169.

Alan Ebnother, *#4*, 2001, photograph by Erika Blumenfeld, P. 170.

Gloria Graham, *FeS2 Pyrite*, 1997, photograph by Erika Blumenfeld, PP. 67, 170.

James Hyde, *Part*, 1993, photograph by Erika Blumenfeld, PP. 78, 171.

Ed Malina, *Untitled*, N.D., photograph by Erika Blumenfeld, P. 172.

John Meyer, *Not titled*, 2001, Egg tempera and lapis lazuli on coated Plexiglas, photograph by Erika Blumenfeld, P. 174.

John Meyer, *Not titled*, 2002, photograph by Erika Blumenfeld, P. 174.

Patricia Moisan, *1624 Heads*, 2002, photograph courtesy Angles Gallery, Santa Monica, California, P. 174.

Leon Polk Smith, *First-One*, 1954, copyright Art © Leon Polk Smith Foundation/Licensed by VAGA, New York, New York, PP. 124, 178.

Leon Polk Smith, *Outer Rim*, 1962, copyright Art © Leon Polk Smith Foundation/Licensed by VAGA, New York, New York, PP. 125, 178.

Heiner Thiel, *MIV/94, #7/9*, 1994, photograph by Erika Blumenfeld; copyright © 2005 Artists Rights Society (ARS), New York/VG Bild-Kunst, Bonn, PP. 126, 178.

Heiner Thiel, *MV/94, e.a., Nr. 2*, 1994, photograph by Erika Blumenfeld; copyright © 2005 Artists Rights Society (ARS), New York/VG Bild-Kunst, Bonn, PP. 127, 178.

Heiner Thiel, *Untitled (Sphere, r=6.6ft.)*, 1998, copyright © 2005 Artists Rights Society (ARS), New York/VG Bild-Kunst, Bonn, PP. 128, 178.

Eric Tillinghast, *#19G*, 1998, photograph by Erika Blumenfeld, P. 179.

Dieter Villinger, *Cadmium Orange*, 1997, copyright © 2005 Artists Rights Society (ARS), New York/VG Bild-Kunst, Bonn, PP. 143, 180.

Dieter Villinger, *Kobaltblau Hell Kobaltblau Turkis*, 1998, copyright © 2005 Artists Rights Society (ARS), New York/VG Bild-Kunst, Bonn, PP. 144, 180.

THE NATALIE AND IRVING FORMAN COLLECTION was designed by Joseph Guglietti in Santa Fe, New Mexico, in collaboration with Karen Lee Spaulding, Deputy Director, Albright-Knox Art Gallery, Buffalo, New York. The texts are set in Adobe Garamond and Frutiger, composed by the designer on an Apple Macintosh. Printed and bound by Transcontinental Printing Inc., Québec City, Canada. Print management provided by Robert L. Freudenheim, Buffalo, New York.